Belle Van Derveer

Soul Waifs

Poems

Belle Van Derveer

Soul Waifs
Poems

ISBN/EAN: 9783744704762

Printed in Europe, USA, Canada, Australia, Japan

Cover: Foto ©Thomas Meinert / pixelio.de

More available books at **www.hansebooks.com**

SOUL WAIFS

Poems

BY
BELLE VAN DERVEER

BUFFALO
THE PETER PAUL BOOK CO
1895

PRINTED AND BOUND BY
THE PETER PAUL BOOK COMPANY,
BUFFALO, N. Y.

To

My Dear Friends

Mr. and Mrs. A. H. Morris

❧

I lovingly inscribe this little volume to you, Mrs. Morris, as a slight token of esteem. You have ever been to me a bright exemplar of all that is good, true, and worthy in womanhood. Your smile, your kindly sympathy, your sweet and unobtrusive philanthropy have lightened the burdens of many, and your mission has ever been to garner souls into the mighty granary of the Lord. Heaven bless you!

I gladly link your name in this dedication, Mr. Morris, for you have ever been a kind, appreciative friend whom to know is to esteem and admire for many rare qualities of heart and mind.

That the Lord may give you both his choicest blessings and length of days, and that our friendship may last till the end of life's journey, is the heartfelt wish of one who can never forget you.

BELLE VAN DERVEER.

PREFACE

The poems in this volume were penned, from time to time, in the few leisure moments of a busy life. Many of them came from the heart in sad hours of grief and gloom, which followed the death of an only son, a lad who was endeared to all who knew him, by his many lovable qualities and noble traits of mind which bespoke a promising future. If any of the lines find a place in the heart of the reader, the author will feel that SOUL WAIFS have not been penned in vain, but will be a bond of sympathy between them henceforth.

THE AUTHOR.

CONTENTS.

Contents

THISTLE DOWN.

FAIRY barques that drift
  Idly here and there ;
Misty sails that catch
  The currents of the air ;
Yet, with rich seed laden
  That shall, haply, grow,—
Where, upon the earth,
  Ah! who may guess or know ?

Airy songs that float
  Carelessly away,
Borne from out the heart,
  Or sorrowful or gay ;
But, the hopes they carry,
  In some life may bloom,
Lessening its pain,
  And lightening its gloom !

13

A HEART'S HISTORY.

ONLY the simple history of a heart,—'tis all,—
    The record of the years that now are past
    and dead,
Yet from whose deeps the phantoms evermore arise
To meet her on life's journey with untold regrets !
They never die — those memories of the golden
    past,
She cannot hush the memories of the far away,
Which like the billows of the troubled sea,
Heard far inland, still voice their sad. eternal woe !
For those who love her, let these lines be penned,
    that when
Her heart is still, and chill this pulse's eager throb,
They may with pity scan this leaflet from the past,
And think of one whose life was but a pleasing
    mask,
Full oft, to hide the fadeless dreams that might have
    been !

Like roses in a garden, sweetly fading, one by one,
The happy years of childhood withered in the
    golden sun !
Then girlhood dawned with all its charm and in-
    finite delight,—
Its vistas garlanded with buds and blossoms ever
    bright !

Oh! could she picture half the joy that blest her
    pathway then,—
The fairy dreams,—the castles reared,—transcend-
    ing tongue or pen !
And lo ! there came a deeper bliss, like an angel
    from above,
It winged into its nest,—her heart, and breathed
    the name of Love !

Then moved she in a realm of sweet enchantment
    all the while ;
She lived, she breathed, but in the halo of his rapt-
    uring smile !
He bore to her the semblance of a being half di-
    vine,—
He was the idol of her soul,—she worshipped at
    his shrine !
Oh, joy ! with sweet responsive glance he looked
    into her eyes !
The thought that he was wholly her's, to her was
    Paradise !
The vision of those blissful days,—how soon it dis-
    appeared !
How soon was torn and scattered all the future love
    had reared !

There came the sad, the parting hour that rested
    like a pall,—
That hour that soon or late must come to crush the
    hearts of all !

She felt that she was dear to him, and, when his
    letters came,
She thought ; nay knew, that in his heart he was to
    her the same.

Years passed away.
        Upon her heart slept one from God,—
A tiny gift that brought a bliss beyond all speech !
A consolation that this earth could not bestow.
And oft as she would gaze into those baby eyes
Would she resolve to live the life allotted her,
And let the Past with all its dreams lie in the grave !
So taking up the burdens of the hour, the seasons
    sped ;
She lived but in the joyous smiles of her sweet
    boy !

She watched him grow with all the hope a mother
    knows ;
He was her thought by day, her dream throughout
    the night !
He was her rose, her gem, her pride, her lovely
    bird !
Alas ! how soon from out her arms he flew away
And left her stunned and speechless in her deathless
    woe !
The seasons wore an alien look since he had flown,
For all that he had looked on, brighter seemed ;
The sun was shut from out the passing day ;

The stars at night were but her darling's watchful
  eyes
That looked upon her from his bright and angel
  home !
Then 'mid the whirlwind of her grief and lone despair
There came a missive from the dead, so seemed it
  then,—
From him whose love had gladdened her in years
  agone !
It whispered hope, it breathed of peace and calmed
  the strife !

Once only had they met, and once his heart had
  striven
To tell its story to her own in burning lines.
Unwedded yet, and but a memory unto her,
That holy love,—then let her here the record keep.

———

O WOULD that heartfelt throbs could talk
    In numbers tried and true,
For language can but feebly mock
    My zealous love for you !

I oft bemoan that cruel fate
    That robbed my jewel dear,
And left my heart most desolate
    With each returning year.

Now oft through memory's horoscope
　　I view those scenes of yore,
When Love's young dream so full of hope
　　Comes back to me once more.

The hours sped by on golden wings,
　　No thought of care had I ;
Thus peace of mind contentment brings
　　When those we love are nigh.

But clouds appeared, the skies o'ercast,
　　In days of long ago,
As when in spring a chilling blast
　　Makes white, fair fields, with snow.

When truth's strong winds those clouds dispersed
　　Love's sun still brighter shone ;
But that fell storm had done its worst,—
　　My fairy bird had flown.

Though many summer suns since then
　　Have wakened into bloom
Erotic life in wood and glen
　　And songs dispelled the gloom ;

Though plumaged birds, inspired to sing,
　　Melodious make the air,
And love, with each returning spring,
　　Makes happy many a pair,

Yet not for me can Nature charm,
  Or melody thrill again,
Since you have left whose skill could calm
  With music's grandest strain.

At length, in Friendship's grasp once more
  We meet, though pressed with care ;
You've trouble seen since days of yore,
  My skies not always fair.

No more returns the dreamland Past,
  Yet haunting memory still
Doth measure well the shadows cast
  On valley, plain and hill.

That joyous time when hope was high,—
  Oh! we were happy then!
When Love's bright dream illumed the sky,—
  The shady wood and glen.

Oh. could Love's dream again return
  With life so fair and gay !
False friends no more would dare to spurn,
  For Love would rule the day !

Maturer life now comes to view ;
  The duty it involves
Shall be my care to honor you
  With manhood's high resolves.

If friends prove false, who favors court,
    One heart shall still prove true,
And e'er through good or ill report,
    Will love and cherish you.

As days go by this thought will cheer
    And life will happier be,
To know, when far away or near,
    You'll sometimes think of me.

Live, sweet, sweet words in memory evermore !
Live in her heart till Life's short span is o'er !
Though wrong has blasted with its crafty hand,
And grief is hers,—Oh, let this record stand
A blissful waif upon Life's wreck-strewn strand !

And thus her heart makes evermore response
To his, and here the record now is set,
That it may haply find him some bright day
When she has gone from earth and all its care,—
When she is but the shadow of a dream,—
E'en as the dream that perished long ago !
Magic spark ! electric flame !
Tell, oh, tell us thy dear name.
Dost thou know thy healing powers?—
How thou cheerest lonely hours?
Wast thou born in heaven above?
Then methinks thy name is Love !
Seventeen,—too young, you think,
To enjoy Love's holy link !

A Heart's History.

Or too weak in intellect,
Too, too fickle to select.
Heart, oh, tell them 'tis untrue,
Love can youngest hearts imbue !
Disappointments desolate
Brought to her the hand of Fate !
'Twas her lot to be thus crushed !
Pangs within her heart were hushed, —
Told to no one save her God !
Was her grief a chastening rod ?

Parted they with sweetest kiss, —
Good-byes spoken, rapturous bliss !
Little thought 'twas time the last, —
And her happiness had past !
Years were hers of grief and joy, —
Had she not an angel boy ?
Sent from heaven to cheer Life's way
Through the dark and dismal day.
How she loved him none can tell,
As his ringing laughter fell
Full of music on her ear,
All the lonely hours to cheer.

Dearer now than aught of earth !
But she never knew his worth,
Till his spirit fled away
Unto realms of perfect day !

She, alone, again was left
Heart-sick and forlorn, bereft!

And she thought of long ago,
Wondering what friend would bestow
Solace in Life's trying hour,—
Who among them had the power,
As the saddened days dragged by,—
Each hour praying God to die !—
Suddenly a thought occurred
And her heart to action stirred.
Caught she then a gleam of light
Through the gloominess of night,
Where was now the friend of yore
Whom she loved long years before?
Would he now to her respond,
And renew their Friendship's bond?
Yes, an answer came ere long,—
Tribute of compassion strong,
Sympathizing with her grief,
Bringing to her soul relief.

Since she'd lost all faith in men,—
"After Death," she asked "what then?"
No hope beyond, tell me your faith
Oh teacher, friend, list what he saith :
"You will find him by and by
Linked by heaven's eternal tie !
Where all partings are unknown,
Where no heart shall say 'Alone !'
Be assured your pure, bright boy
Idol of your heart, and joy,

Has escaped life's sins and strife,
Now translated to that life
Where he'll welcome parents dear,
Nevermore to shed a tear."

Blessed words, they deeply sank
As with yearning soul she drank ;
Consolation thus expressed
Soothed all her aching breast !

Fourteen years of hope deferred,—
Fourteen years since she had heard
From that friend of long ago,—
Now she questioned why 'twas so,
Soon an answer came again,
Eased once more her silent pain.

What rich treasures Memory holds,—
Of what " might have been " enfolds !
For the clasp and thrill of Love
Now unto her Life are wove !
And no more she feels alone
While he lives whose manly tone
Can inspire her to awake
And, anew, great courage take !
Looking forward, she'll press on
Hoping for some brighter dawn,
Separated though they are,
Hope's bright orb still gleams afar,

And, though they should never meet
Winter's cold nor summer's heat,
Now can make her heart forget,
While the stars are heavenward set !

Prayers now nightly shall ascend
For his welfare, trusted friend !
Guardian angels, watch thou near,
Look thou down with pitying ear !
Hearken, Father, throned above,
Hear her prayer, *Thy* name is Love !

Only the simple history of a heart, 'tis all,—
Out of the Past, fond memories to recall !

QUEENA.

I.

A FAIR young girl is bending o'er the picture of
a youth,
She gazes at it with delight, with lovelit eyes of
truth ;
She speaks to it with tenderness, with innocence
and joy,
Alas ! that one sad word of pain hope's future
should destroy.

II.

So earnestly she gazes on that face, she does not
see
The living face that watches from the doorway
eagerly,
A face that bears in lividness the message of a doom,
That comes to cloud life's sunshine with its bitter,
bitter gloom.

III.

She meets his glance, and shyly, with a pretty
charming grace,
She strives to hide the picture, can her throbbing
heart not trace

Within those pallid features as she murmurs Walter
    dear?
And clings with all a woman's love, the parting
    hour is near?

IV.

Oh darling, I've a message from my father o'er the
    sea,
I go to him to-morrow, 'though my heart I leave
    with thee;
Cheer up; 'tis but a little while and we shall meet
    again,
Oh drive from out those tender eyes that look of
    fear and pain.

V.

Yes, soon I will return, and we then need no more
    conceal
The holy ties that bind us, I'll to the world re-
    veal;
I'll claim thee as my wedded wife, cheer up then,
    Queena mine;
My father will receive you, all is well, do not re-
    pine.

VI.

The sunset's dying gleam shone o'er a fallen figure
    there,
And on the passing breeze there rang a wild cry of
    despair.

Afar across the sea he sails, the husband of her
    heart,
God's pity on the love that sees its idol thus de-
    part.

VII.

Six years have winged their flight above life's
    dreary tangled maze,
All Paris now is ringing with a fair young singer's
    praise,
And Queena is the lyric soul that stirs the city
    grand,
And brings her subjects to her feet with song's
    august command.

VIII.

The rich, the titled 'round her throng ; and one, a
    marquis great,
Proffers his mansion for her home and all his vast
    estate ;
With Queena, goes a lovely child to share this pal-
    ace home,
Her mother's ward she says to those, who ques-
    tion while they roam.

IX.

But who is this approaching her and clinging to
    his side,
A stately proud young lady who is soon to be his
    bride?

'Tis Walter : As she gazes on that face to her unkind
She cries, as she beholds his eyes : " My God, he's
  blind ; he's blind !"

X.

The gloom of death fall's 'round her, but a strong
  will conquers all,
And soon the old familiar voice her senses now
  enthrall.
" Mam'selle, the language of sweet flowers, pray tell
  me do you know ?
This rose, an emblem of my friendship, let me
  thus bestow.

XI.

" Your voice, oh Madamoiselle Reni, doth remind
  me of a voice
That I have heard in other years that made my
  heart rejoice ;
If I could only look upon your face, it must be fair,
For all the goodness of your heart I know is written there.

XII.

"A sense of sweet contentment, do I feel when by
  your side,"—
Alas, for poor, poor Queena, how her heart was
  sorely tried ;

But soon the strains of music ushered in the merry
    dance,
And then to claim her lover did the beauty proud
    advance ;

XIII.

Her dimpled arms she placed in Walter's with a
    peerless grace,
Lord Huntington, it was his son, as if it were her
    place ;
Oh cruel was the pain that Queena felt at this sad
    hour,
And oh the woe, the agony, that were her wifely
    dower.

XIV.

The beauty spoke of one, a poor and humble
    country girl
Whom Walter knew in years gone by, she spoke
    with lips that curl ;
Then Queena tore a locket from her breast and
    shouted, " See : "
" I show her face to you ! " and laughed out scorn-
    fully.

XV.

" Oh God ! I'm mad ! " she shouted to that wild,
    excited throng.
The beauty said, " These arms unto the Hunting-
    ton's belong ; "

Then spake my Lord, " This cannot be." " 'Tis
    true," poor Queena cried,
" Six years ago your son gave this to me, I was
    his bride !

XVI.

" America, that is my home, and there we twain
    were wed,
'Though secretly, yet soon from me your son was
    hither led,
And this the locket was a pledge forevermore to be
Of our God-hallowed union in that fair land of the
    free."

XVII.

Poor creature, she is mad, they cried, then toward
    the door she swept,
" Who says that I am mad, Oh God !" In
    agony she wept ;
" What eyes are those that burn into my own so
    wildly sad,
Heaven help me now, yes I'm mad, yes mad, I
    am mad."

XVIII.

Then breathless and amazed were all. She flung
    at Walter's feet
The locket which had been his gift when life to her
    was sweet.

Back to her quiet home she fled, pressed to her
    heart their child
Who vainly called for papa 'mid her tears of an-
    guish wild.

XIX.

Then, as she sat and lonely read the papers which
    had rent
The bonds that were between them, by her misery
    o'erbent,
A step approached, a voice she knew so sweetly
    called her name,
"O, Queena, see, on bended knee, forgive me, do
    not blame!"

XX.

She spurned him. "Leave me, sir," she cried.
    "This paper tells you all.
Our lives are severed evermore, love gone beyond
    recall."
Then through the doorway came their little child,
    so sweet, so fair!
"Take papa back for my sake, mamma," fell those
    accents there.

XXI.

"Forgive me, for I read your death in lands be-
    yond the sea.
Oh, cast me not from out your heart; dear
    Queena, speak to me.

But sorrow and deep suffering all these years I've
    seen,
And like a wanderer from sweet heaven all these
    days I've been.

XXII.

"Do you recall the rose-bush that we planted?"
    then he said.
"Its roses, like our love," wept Queena, "long
    ago they fled."
"No, Queena, no; we thought it died, but like
    our love, my own,
'Tis strengthened and 'tis nourished by the storms
    that it hath known."

XXIII.

"O, here's a rose I culled from it; a token may it
    be
Of our new love, God grant that it may bloom
    eternally."
Their little child joined both their hands, and all the
    clouds had passed,
And thus to Queena, out of tempest came her joy
    at last!

INSPIRATION.

O, BEAUTIFUL Goddess, come aid me to
muse !
Still into my heart thy blest spirit infuse,
Now, over my being waft holiest power,
For in my sad life thou dost lighten each hour.

Thou comest unseen, but thy mantle we feel,
As into our heart thou dost silently steal ;
So calmly thy pinions are hovering near,
Inspiring our moments with heavenly cheer !

Delay not ! I wait thee ! Oh, haste to me now !
At the shrine of thy power, thus humbly I bow !
I longingly sigh for thy whisper of love,
Oh, come, gentle Goddess, like balm from above!

Then bear me still onward to yon blest abode,
While I list to the strains of thy heavenly ode !
For in yon mystic realm ever rock me to sleep,
Where hosts of the angels thy harp-strings now
sweep !

Lo ! Angelic spirits are hovering round !
For blest peace and comfort the moments have
crowned ;

And e'en from the bitterest hour of a life
Thy whispers have banished the care and the strife.

I feel that the hand which is tracing this line
Is guided by heavenly powers divine !
I know that an influence, hallowed and pure,
Is bidding me teach other hearts to endure !

Without thy sweet influence, thy power divine,
Our words are but meaningless, dear Goddess
    mine !
And e'en though our conscience prompt to good
    deeds,
Thy spirit 'tis guides us, and answers our needs.

All life with thy magical power is blest !
It hallows our labor and beautifies rest !
It gilds every moment with loving delight,
And brightens the soul, as the stars do the night.

Oh, thankfully ever thy joys we receive !
Be swift in thy visits,—be slow us to leave !
We yearn for thy influence earnest and strong ;
Oh, come, gentle Goddess, with rapturous song !

LIGHT OF MY LIFE!

LIGHT of my Life! I groped in cheerless
  dark,
  Until thy smile first dawned on me!
My heart the dove, and thine the ark,
  Upon the tossed and troubled sea!
          Light of my Life!

I looked to thee for Hope, for Peace,
  And found these in thine arms again!
The cares of day had then surcease,
  And fled the anguish and the pain,—
          Light of my Life!

One thought alone lives in my heart,—
  One wish,—to thee enfold!
To speak these words : " No more apart
  We'll bide!" Oh, bliss untold,—
          Light of my Life!

Oh, live the time ; 'twill not be late
  Ere God shall join a love so true!
My soul still pleads at heaven's gate,
  That soon we may not say adieu !—
          Light of my Life!

HEART LONGINGS.

OH, how we reach our hands to grasp
    Food for the hungry soul !
We hope and yearn and wish and wait,
    While years so swiftly roll !

We know that earth will pass away,
    We sigh for something real ;
Oh, what is that for which we long,—
    The soul's far-off ideal ?

We still can taste the joys of earth,
    But our hunger will return !
There's something always gleams afar
    For which the heart will yearn !

The sweetest music we can hear,
    In symphony and song ;
But hearts will yearn for something still,
    Till they to Christ belong !

When we have given all to Him,
    We never know a fear !
He leads us gently by the hand,
    He ever lingers near !

His gospel is the richest feast !
  It fills the hungry heart !—
And while we journey on our way
  Becomes of life a part !

Ah ! still he calls : " Come unto Me !
  And I will give you rest ! "
He guideth us, Oh, longing heart,
  To that sweet Home so blest !

A WEDDING RHYME.

MISS MOLLIE DEVENDORF.   DR. BRAHMAN MEDING.

FROM this canopy bright of fair daisies,
  May your lives that now mingle glide on,
Like a violet, through woodland mazes,
  Till the great sea before you is won !

As the sun gleameth softly this morning.
  May the moments of life ever shine ;
And each day be a bridal-day dawning,
  With a hope and a love still divine !

Though the daisies may wither and perish,
  There are blossoms deep down in the heart
That the dew of affection will cherish,—
  That will sweetness forever impart !

May the fair silken ties that now bind you,
  Clasp you stronger as time glides away,
May the sunbeams of life ever find you ;
  Strewn with daisies be each passing day !

PHŒBE.

FOR A CHILD.

WHEN leaves hang listlessly, at noon,
  And even bees forget to croon,
A plaintive voice calls, soft and low,
"Phœbe!"—Would you the story know?

Two tiny girls, set out, one day,
For school, but wildflowers whispered, "Play!"
A merry brook sang, "Follow me!
These woods have splendid sights to see.
We'll ramble through these fair green dells,
And search for lovely lily-bells.
See! here are nice stones for your feet;
Cross over, never fear, my sweet!"

Lo each, unthinking, crossed the brook,
And strayed from mossy nook to nook,
And listened to the leaves that spoke,
In whispers, from the bending oak;
And saw, from thick-leaved bushes near,
Shy birds peep out and at them peer,
As if to say: "What birds are these?
We'll trill a song their ears to please."

39

'Tis said a fairy happened by,
And two young sleepers chanced to spy ;
For they were wearied out with fun,
And warm and drowsy grew the sun.
"Ho! Ho!" winked he, "intruders here?
Truants from school, that's very clear.
I'll wake them up ; a trick! a trick!
I'll play upon them," quoth he, "quick!
They'd make nice birds, upon my word!"
A touch,—and each woke up a bird!
They hopped away, and flew o'erhead
Where sunlit boughs above them spread.
They dipped their soft wings in the stream,
And fluttered in its diamond gleam.
They reveled in the sweet, blue sky,—
Flew, as the other birdies fly ;
But, ere the dewy twilight fell,
They'd lost each other in the dell ;
And all night long they'd pined alone,
And when the early morning shone,
Each called the other pleadingly,
From bush to bush, from tree to tree.
And that's the reason, I've heard say,
A bird calls "Phœbe!" to this day.

UNFORGOTTEN.

TO MY FRIEND, MRS. H. J. S.   IN MEMORY OF
HER HUSBAND.

THOUGH long years have passed, beloved,
  Since from me you went away,
Yet you still are unforgotten,
  Even for a single day !

'Twas the deepest love that bound us,
  Heart to heart, and mind to mind ;
Thoughts of you are all that cheer me,—
  All the joy on earth I find !

Husband mine, methinks your spirit
  Hovers near, at starry eve,
Bringing to me precious comfort,—
  Bidding me no more to grieve !

We have strewn sweet garlands o'er you,
  Watered with our blinding tears ;
We have sought the mound that hides you,
  All these sad and lonely years.

Oh, yon resting place is sacred !
  You have seemed so near me there !
I have hallowed it with roses,
  Lilies bright and pure and fair.

Through the mists and shadows lead me
    To that Home of peace above,
Where again we'll be united
    By our God whose name is Love !

Unforgotten is that memory,
    Still to me a priceless gem !
Fadeless as the rays that sparkle
    In an angel's diadem !

Oh, the child of our adoption,
    Who has well repaid our care,
Walks with me life's path, to meet you,
    In our Father's mansion fair !

"OH! FOR THE TOUCH OF A VANISHED HAND!"

"OH! for the touch of a vanished hand,
  The sound of a voice that is still!"
We're longing to meet that silent band,
  Who bowed to the Father's will!

Oh, sacred sorrow! Oh, wretched gloom!—
  The shadow and pall of death!
We follow our loved ones to the tomb,
  While we gaze with bated breath.

The death of a loved one, gone to God,
  Seems a dreaded theme to some!
They cannot see the chastening rod,
  Their hearts seem cold and dumb.

Those who passed away, within the vale,
  Anchored with faith so sure,
Will nevermore feel earth's stormy gale,
  In that heavenly land so pure!

To-day we would lay a tribute there,
  O'er the graves of our loved so dear;
And courage take, our cross to bear,
  And be brave, for God is near.

When with a loved one we're called to part,
   On earth to meet nevermore,
It touches a deeper chord in the heart—
   Than ever was stirred before.

'Tis then that the cry comes to one and all
   To awake to a nobler life ;
To list to the spirit's warning call,
   And fearlessly meet the strife.

Hark ! from the beautiful gates ajar
   We can hear loved voices float ;
And, in that music borne afar,
   Our loved sing the sweetest note !

Let us be led by the vanished hand,
   It must beckon us not in vain ;
For in that beautiful summer land
   We shall meet all our loved again !

TWO IN ONE.

TWO clouds of yonder tranquil sky,
  In peaceful motion met my gaze ;
They glided onward, each drew nigh,
  Until, at last, their mingled rays
    Sparkled in glories all divine !
    Oh, such thy Life and mine !

Alone I walked the road of Life,
Endured its bitterness and strife ;
A light shone on my troubled way,
And Lo ! the darkness turned to day ! —
    It was the light of Love divine, —
    Oh, such thy Love and mine !

I saw two buds, at Springtime's glow
  Come forth to beautify the earth ;
They grew, as hearts together grow,
  At Love's all-hallowed, rapturous birth !
    Until a blended rose both shine, —
    Oh, thus thy heart and mine !

I LONG FOR THOSE BRIGHT EYES!

THE roses long, in Summer sweet,
  For dew-drops, pearly fair ;
The brooklet sighs the sea to meet,—
  Its fond embrace to share ;
Fond hearts that day has parted here—
  Oft yearn for starry skies ;
But evermore, till Life is o'er,
  I long for those bright eyes !

I care not for the sunlit sheen
  That broods o'er vales and hills ;
Or zephyrs, fragrant and serene,
  That dimple all the rills ;
The glory of the sunset hour
  Of wondrous tints and dyes,—
Over my heart these have no power,—
  I long for those bright eyes !

I long for them, when Life grows sad
  With overclouding care ;
I long for them, when bright and glad
  The world seems everywhere !
Whate'er the years may bring to me,
  One thought will still arise :
I long, dear heart, thy face to see,—
  I long for those bright eyes !

NOT ALONE.

NOT alone. Ah ! not alone,
   When I can think of friends my own !
Though absent from my sight, my heart
Still in their being has its part.
Each image ever present seems,
Each lives in all my hopes, my dreams ;
In Fancy falls each voice's tone,
Though parted, I am not alone,—
         Ah ! not alone.

Not alone, when I recall
Those tender words were wont to fall,—
Those smiles that never failed to cheer,
And lighter made Life's burdens drear.
The star of Hope still fondly shines,
And Memory still round thee twines ;
Oh, since bright eyes have on me shone,
I nevermore can be alone,—
         Ah ! not alone.

Not alone,—I know that thou,
Dear friend, art thinking of me now !
A golden thread of sympathy,
Through space unites my heart to thee !

47

And so a weary Life is blest
For thou art still my hourly guest !
We ne'er may meet, 'till the unknown,
And yet, I ne'er can be alone,—
          Ah ! not alone.

AUTUMN.

AS the leaves are slowly fading,—
    Leaves of purple, red and gold,
Sorrow is my spirit shading,
    And an anguish all untold !

Oh, the winds, so chill and dreary,
    Heralding the ermine snow !
Echoed in my heart so weary
    After Summer's golden glow !

Yet, there is a voice that telleth :
    " Look beyond this dearth and Death !
God through clouds of Winter dwelleth
    As He does through Summer's breath !"

FOREVERMORE.

NO other word from out my heart
    Can all its eloquence impart ;
There is no word that can express
My soul's dear joy and happiness,
Like this one that I murmur o'er,—
    Forevermore ! Forevermore !
    Thine, thine, forevermore !

In all of Life's vicissitudes,
Where woe so oft on bliss intrudes ;
In every heart-throb that one thought
Sets every other—yea, as naught !
My boundless Hope it doth restore !
    Forevermore ! Forevermore !
    Thine, thine, forevermore !

What are the days of suffering,
And all that loneliness may bring ?
One hope, one blissful hope is mine,
When stars no more for me will shine,
We'll meet on yon celestial shore,—
    Forevermore ! Forevermore !
    Thine, thine, forevermore !

WHERE'ER I GO.

I CANNOT lose thee from mine eyes !
　　I gaze upon the sea,
When stars begem the purpled skies,—
　　Each star recalls but thee !
I listen to the waves that sigh
　　Along the snow-white shore ;
Thy name, they breathe, soft rippling by,
　　　　Forevermore !

The first sweet buds of Spring unfold
　　Thy fairness to my sight ;
In leaves of crimson and of gold
　　I read thy glorious light !
Among the crowd of busy streets
　　I greet thee o'er and o'er ;
An inward voice thy name repeats,—
　　　　Forevermore !

There is no day, in storm or shine,
　　When thou'rt remembered not !
My dearest hopes 'round thee entwine,—
　　Thou ne'er shalt be forgot !
And all through God's eternity,
　　When earth for us is o'er,
My Heaven shall be in loving thee,—
　　　　Forevermore !

ONLY A WORD.

ONLY a word as light as air !
But oh, a heart it broke,
A spirit glad, a home so fair,
To pain and sadness woke !

Only a word,—to ban, to bless,
It falls, from hour to hour ;
A boon of untold tenderness,
A curse of mighty power.

Only a word, a heart in woe
Came back to joy, to life !
It brought to cheeks the brightened glow,
And hushed the bosom's strife.

Only a word, a path was turned
That led to darkest sin,—
A reckless soul its mission learned
Life's heritage within !

Only a word,—two hearts are one !
That listened there and heard ;
Two paths in Love forever run,
Because of that sweet word !

THE LILIES.

OH, lilies in your loveliness,
    I gazed on you in dreams,
Before the sunlight came to bless,
    And wake you with its beams !
Your simple beauty seemed to say :
    " We bloom for all below,
And shall they not sweet homage pay
    Ere winds of winter blow ? "

Oh, lilies, in your peaceful smile
    I saw the smile of One,
The Pure, the Holy, past all guile,
    God's well-beloved Son !
For has He not extolled your grace
    Of all the flowers that grow ?
Within my heart I keep a place
    For you, oh, flowers of snow !

LITTLE WHITE GRAVE.

LITTLE white grave, oh, silently there,
    A solemn story you tell :
Of hopes and burdens so bitter to bear,
    Breathing a deep mournful knell.
Saddened our hearts, to look on thee
    What anguish untold we share ;
Merciful God, oh, can it be
    Our darling is resting there?

CHORUS.

Good-bye, dear little sacred spot,
    Beneath the clinging vine,
Oh it shalt never be forgot,—
    Blest little grave of thine !
We know that winter cometh soon,
    With ermine frosts and snow,
This vine will twine one little boon
    O'er thy dear grave so low !

Bright angel child, why could we not keep
    Thee here in our earthly home?
Oh, darling, we now so bitterly weep,
    With hearts all sad and lone ;
These pure white flowers will silently tell
    Of thy own pure life, my boy,

53

Emblem to us, who loved thee so well,
  Of heavenly peace and joy.

CHORUS:—

I eagerly listen ; the message I hear,
  " A little child ever shall lead,"
'Mid storms and darkness this thought shall
      cheer,—
  Assurance most blessed indeed.
Can all this toil and talent be lost ?
  Are earthly hopes withered dreams ?
But though on life's dark billows we're tossed
  One ray o'er our path still gleams.

CHORUS:—

Saviour, our trust now on Thee is stayed,
  Thou wilt make all plainer at last ;
Our burden-bearer Thou truly wast made,
  All sorrows will soon, soon be past.
Then lead Thou on, Choir Master divine,
  Our Hope through time Thou shalt be ;
We hear now Thy call, we bow at Thy shrine,
  Lead on we will follow Thee.

CHORUS:—

THOUGHTS ON THE BIBLE.

A WONDERFUL book is the Book of Life,—
    Its treasures how vast to define !
'Tis our God revealing to all mankind
    His message of grandeur sublime !

Its language prophetic, the soul of truth,
    Recorded by hearts that were pure ;
Inspired with power from Him on high,
    Thus, one with His name, to endure !

One Author dictated who rules us all,
    Infusing His utterance therein ;
The Holy Spirit directed His work
    To shield us from sorrow and sin !

And, methinks when God wrote the final word,
    He said to the angelic fold,—
" Let all the nations of earth rejoice,
    Though half of My glory's untold ! "

And when the great work was completed there,
    What loud hallelujahs were sung ;
For marvelous works were therein revealed
    For nations of every tongue !

Surely one proof of this Book is the Church,
    Its protection so strong and true,—
Its foundation sure, like a wall built round,
    Spreading faith ever old, yet new !

We're sure God Almighty inspired the Book,
    Because 'tis the food of the soul !
As true as the very air we breathe,
    Enduring while planets roll !

Who could have forseen in that dark age ;
    When idolatry reigned around,
Excepting the high, the holiest one
    To whom our lives should be bound ?

The Being who wrote that first great command,
    The human heart also did make ;
Our minds can conceive his wondrous works,
    And to nobler life we awake !

Oh ! birds of the morn that heavenward fly,
    What a difference 'twixt you and me !
Your grief is so short, while we cannot forget,
    While we're mourning continually.

But we know our Father hath given command
    To us "to serve Him alone !
Before me no other Gods thou shalt have !"
    His will, ever be our own !

And again we open His Book, and read :
    If we wish our days long in the land,
Our parents dear we must honor and love,
    Thus keeping His precept grand.

From Genesis on to the end of the Book
    Oh ! what strains of divine command !
God leading nations, with power supreme,
    To the beautiful Promised Land !

The Book stands unchallenged for Truth, to-day !
    When this world was formed, none can tell ;
" In the beginning was Light !" God said
    'Tis sufficient, and all is well !

It may have stood millions of years or more,
    Geology proves it to-day ;
So "in the beginning," whenever it was,
    We accept it, and who would say nay ?

Now, of inspiration, some do not believe ;
    Not many we know have possessed
This infusion divine with its power sublime,
    Very few have by it been blessed.

Just now this great truth is forced on our mind
    By the little boy Hoffmann to-day ;
For he follows in harmony grand, Mozart,
    With music's all powerful sway.

And Webster, too, with his mental force
  Superior to friends or kin ;
A great power guided his work on earth,
  Vast knowledge from him we win.

And Franklin caught the electric spark
  From the canopied, starry sky !
Thus connecting earth, from shore to shore,
  Almost reaching to worlds on high.

It was softly whispered in Edison's ear
  To invent the great telephone ;
Linking the thoughts of the world by its power
  As they travel from zone to zone !

Some say, "who is He," and "where is this
    God?"
  "God is thought !" thus Harzal doth say ;
Spencer says "Unknowable !" Carlyle "Force!"
  Put we such thoughts far away !

God is a Spirit I read to-day,
  My Saviour, guardian and friend ;
The Bread of Life to His children dear
  Forevermore He doth send !

GRANDPA'S VISION.

WHILST I on my pillow was lying,
    On last Decoration Day eve,
The whispering breeze, softly sighing,
    Seemed bidding my soul not to grieve.

A vision was hovering o'er me,—
    A rapturous vision of Peace;
No worldly thought lingered before me,
    Each care had a restful release.

Then, as the sweet vision came nearer,
    My Georgie's bright face I could see,
Which now unto me was much dearer,
    Than all this world's glory could be!

A whisper, as loving eyes met me,
    With sweetest of smiles on his face,—
" Dear grandpa, I ne'er can forget thee,
    E'en though in this heavenly place !"

With angel arms now he enfolds me,
    And stamps his sweet kiss on my brow;
His presence celestial now holds me,
    And comfort to me doth endow !

A myth, or a dream, or a spirit,—
  Oh, call it whatever you may !
'Twas joy beyond life to be near it,
  And it lighted my heart with its ray !

Sweet vision, come oft to caress me !
  Enfold your bright wings o'er my life !
And with your fond kisses oft bless me,
  And scatter the darkness and strife !

My old heart is sure you are treasured
  And safe from the world's weary care;
God's love which surrounds you, *unmeasured*,
  Ah, how could I wish you not there !

Safe, safe in that bright home above us,
  All sheltered from sorrow and sin,
We know that you tenderly love us,—
  God's angels have folded you in !

    *   *   *   *   *

Only one year ago to-night,—
  Ah, grandpa's blue-eyed boy,
How brave you spoke for truth and right,—
  Your mother's hope and joy !

I never shall forget your face,
  That beamed with looks so bright,
As you came forth, with manly grace,
  Last Decoration night !

Alas! that in so short a time
    You in the grave were laid !
And there, in glory's peaceful clime,
    With angels are arrayed !

But sad and lonely though we are,
    This Decoration Eve,
We hearken to a voice afar
    Which bids us ne'er to grieve !

Oh, as we list, we'll courage take,
    And say '' God's will be done !''
Trying on earth this life to make
    A holy, useful one !

To-day we lingered o'er your grave,
    That hallowed, quiet spot !
While flowers were strewn o'er soldiers brave,
    We could forget you not !

And so we brought sweet buds to-day,
    And scattered them around:
Oh, did you see, from far away,
    That peaceful burial mound ?

We made a beauteous bower there,
    Above your resting place;
We strewed the garlands sweet and fair
    Above your precious face !

And while with saddened hearts we prayed,
   Low bending o'er your mound,
Your spirit then we knew had strayed
   From Heaven, and us had found !

And meet it seemed to decorate
   Your little grave with flowers,
Who spake for right, with boyhood's might,
   Oh, soldier dear of ours !

TIME.

SIT'ST thou idly asking why
   Time so swiftly passes by ?
Can we buy a month or year ?
Could we call back moments dear ?
No! the moments precious, fly,
Tick by tick, they wander by !
Idle not, then, one bright hour,
Time is still Life's grandest dower.
Transient, fleeting, at its best,
Voyage on Life's ocean breast;
As we softly downward glide
With the hand of Time to guide.
What though Time doth changes bring,
Wounds us with his cruel sting ?

He doth also try to heal,
And with mortals gently deal.
When he e'en takes *all* away,—
All that made life bright and gay,—
Welcome is his quickened pace.
For we'll soon have won our race !
Who would call him back again,
With his hours of silent pain?
Rather speed him in his flight
Than recall one heart-worn fight !
For, as sure as Life begins,
'Tis a fight to him who wins !
And, when on our couch we lie,
When we say: "Old Time, good-by !"
When we reach yon fairer clime,
Then, perhaps we'll know thee, Time !

TO MOTHER.

EVER the same the river flows;
　Ever the same is childhood's mirth;
Ever the same the sunset glows;
　Ever the same is Springtime's birth.

Ever the same is Summer's flight;
　Ever the same are stars above;
Ever the same are Truth and Right,
　Ever the same is Mother's love !

FIVE LITTLE LEAVES.

FOR A CHILD.

FIVE little leaves, one autumn day,
  Set out to have a sail;
They met a brook upon their way,
  As they danced before the gale.

Their names were, Purple, Gold and Brown,
  And Red, and Crimson bright;
They whispered, "We'll go floating down,
  But all come back ere night.

"Stop, silver brook! we'll go along:"
  The brook said ne'er a word,
Although it lisped a warning song
  These silly leaves ne'er heard.

"Oh, pretty leaves, your mother-tree
  You never will see more,
If you go sailing down with me,—
  You'd better stay on shore!"

Five little leaves went sailing by,
  Like fairy boats were they;
The autumn sun as yet was high,
  The night was far away.

They saw no more the mother-tree !
And, if you'll go and look,
Like jewels, every one you'll see
Deep down within the brook !

MY DEAREST HEART.

THE days were dark before you brought me
   gladness,
   But in your smiles I saw the beaming sun !
The clouds no more enfold my soul in sadness,
   The storms that filled my way are past and done.
You came to bless and comfort me forever,
   Your glances whisper: " Love, we ne'er shall
      part !"
Each thought is yours, and not e'en Death can
   sever
   Our paths, my dearest heart, my dearest heart !

I sighed for you, through days of hopeless sorrow;
   At last, we met, as true hearts always meet !
The past was dead, and joy illumed each morrow,
   For in your eyes I read love's lesson sweet !
You came to me when every link seemed broken;
   The years were long that kept our lives apart !
But now you're mine by every tender token,
   My own,—my dearest heart, my dearest heart !

I fear no more the future's way before me,
   While you may walk, an angel, by my side !
The star of Hope is fondly shining o'er me,
   And down the stream of Time we'll softly glide.
Within your eyes I see but rapture gleaming,
   It bids each shadow from my life depart !
The light of love for me is ever beaming,
   My joy,—my dearest heart, my dearest heart !

THANKSGIVING.

HOW matchless are Thy mercies Lord !
   How boundless is Thy love !
With grateful hearts we bow to Thee,
   Our King enthroned above.
We sing Thy praise with thankfulness ;
   Thy grace, oh, may we share !
Can we forget Thy benefits,—
   Thy kindly guardian care ?

Though many, bowed with hopeless grief,
   Thy power cannot define,
We recognize the hand that smites
   As Wisdom most divine.
Thy tenderness, oh, may we prise,
   And say "Thy will be done !"
Still may we look through darkest night
   And see Hope's radiant sun.

Thanks for the earth whereon we live,—
 Our joys, our loved ones near.
Thanks for the blessings Thou hast showered
 With each returning year.
Thanks for the Saviour Thou hast given,
 With humbleness we pray,
And offer up our thanks to Thee
 This blest Thanksgiving day.

THROUGH DARK, TO LIGHT.

"BE Thou the Judge, oh, God!" I prayed,
 Nor was Thine answer long delayed.
For soon the shadows that were thrown,
Above my earthly way, had flown.
Amid the blackness of the night,
Behold anew Thy glorious light.

Thy hand, oh, Saviour, leads the way
From darkness to the perfect day.
God's shadows were to try my soul,
Till won, at last, the Heavenly goal.
With thankful heart I give Thee praise,
Oh, Father, all my earthly days!

'Tis through the burden and the Cross,—
The pain, the sorrow, and the loss,—

The spirit tried, as though by fire,
That onward, upward, hearts aspire.
" Be Thou the Judge !" I prayed to Thee,
Oh, God, and Thou hast answered me !

SEPARATION.

HOW long the hours until we meet,
    How slowly pass the day and night.
There is no bloom in summer sweet,
    Unshared with thee, my hope my light.

I tell Love's story o'er and o'er,
    In words that thou hast breathed to me ;
My heart but loves thee more and more
    While absence keeps my days from thee.

The flowers repeat in fragrance rare
    The utterance of thy dear eyes ;
In every thought, and wish, and prayer,
    In dawn and radiant sunset skies,—

Thy face appears, to bless and cheer,
    And yet, my heart is lone and sad,
My all of joy is when thou'rt near ;
    In thy sweet glance, alone, I'm glad.

Oh, Love ! Immortal, hallowed love !
    How can I bide the hours of gloom ?

I watch the tranquil stars above,
　　And wonder why 'tis Love's sad doom

To linger, heart from heart, so long,
　　For thy sweet presence makes to me,
In every moment, one fond song ;
　　Life, bliss and rapturous melody.

Oh, cross of love that we must bear !
　　Dark separation's ceaseless pain,
Until thy smiles again I share,
　　Until, my own, we meet again.

We said good-bye, with lips that met,
　　In one long kiss of lingering bliss ;
How often since when last we met
　　I've lived again that rapturous kiss.

There is no hour when thou art not
　　Beside me, in sweet Fancy's dream ;
No word of thine can he forgot,—
　　Of Hope, thou art my only gleam.

The Past, for both, has known its pain,
　　But in the Future there must be
All Joy, all Life, all Hope ; and fain
　　My heart would these be unto thee.

Then why should separation make
　　Sad hours? I know that we shall meet,
And for thy love,—thy dear love's sake,
　　Thy gentle arms shall clasp me, sweet !

MISJUDGED.

HOW oft the world will wrongly scan each
    action,
  With busy eye, malignant and severe,
And prove, unto its own sweet satisfaction,
  That right is wrong, by argument most clear !

The fairest flower for a weed is taken,
  The breath of slander blights a heart most true;
And e'en a life that strives all good to waken
  How many round us ever misconstrue !

Oh, heed the precept of divine affection :
  Judge not! ye ne'er can know another's heart ;
The secret springs of life are past inspection;
  Only to self can self its aims impart.

Thy brother and thy sister speak of kindly,
  While o'er the rugged road of life ye plod;
Ah, judge them not, all partially and blindly;
  Watch well thyself, and leave the rest to God.

SUFFER LITTLE CHILDREN.

WE yield them up with anguished hearts,
    With weary, weeping eyes;
We gaze within the narrow graves,
    The gates of Paradise.
But heart, there softly comes to thee,
"Suffer them now to come to me."

Oh, blessed balm for motherhood,
    What storms can harm them now?
They sing the Saviour's endless praise,
    While sadly here we bow,
God's jewels, in His crown to be,
"Forbid not, let them come to me."

Take up the burden of thy cross
    For unto thee 'tis given
To render thy sad earthly life
    More meet for yonder heaven.
Dear Christ, Thy goodness now we see
"Suffer thou them to come to me!"

SUNLIGHT FOR WORKINGMEN.

WHEN the sun rises golden to bring us the
day,
Awakening all who are plodding life's way,
What myriads then to their labor must throng,
With a frown or a sigh, or a smile and a song.

There are many lives weary and worn with their
toil,
The tenders of ships and the tillers of soil;
What beautiful thoughts of theirs' crowded away
In the dull round of routine that shadows the day.

How many with minds of ambition rejoice
In the task and the toil of their option and choice;
How many are giving their labor for all,
With hearts still responding to mercy's loud call.

Then how many are searching for pleasures to-day,
In Fashion's great world all resplendent and gay;
But the nymph glideth by, oft refusing the call,
Her flatteries never were destined for all.

All in vain is the search over land, over sea,
In the midst of the garlands of pleasure and glee,
For the heart its true happiness never can find
While selfishness rules the domain of the mind.

Oh, the time has gone by to grind earthward the
    poor,
They have trials and troubles enough to endure;
We're living and breathing in more hopeful days,
And life has a vastly more generous phase.

Oh, the sweet loving children who gather around,
The bright golden links of our home, rapture-
    crowned!
What glory of sunlight their clear laughter brings,
And how long in the heart-core its melody rings.

They have hopes that are greater than those in far
    lands,
While here they are reared by kind, toil-faring
    hands;
The highest of places awaits for them here,
As they strive after wisdom, from year unto year.

Oh, toil-wearied brothers, take courage to-day ;
The clouds that o'erhang you will soon fade away ;
The sunlight is coming, to cheer you, at last,
The strife and the bitterness soon will be past.

The fiat goes forth, by the might of your hands
The vistas of progress opes now through the lands;
Yield not in the conflict, let none give up heart,
Your own conscience dictates the bold, hero part.

Prosperity's banner will over you wave,—
Your homes and your firesides from misery save;
A blessing, all equal, and sunlight sublime,
Shall fall on the workingman, fadeless through
    time.

SPRINGTIME VOICES.

DO you know, O, happy bluebirds,
    That I've guessed your silver song?
That I read the loving message
    Of your hearts, so blithe and strong?
On your tiny wings of turquois,
    Flashing by, you carol clear:
"'Tis the Giver of the Springtime
    Who has sent us earth to cheer."

I can hear it in the brooklet
    That is laughing down the lea,
Like a merry little baby
    From its cradle-bed set free.
And the crocus and the daisy,
    Lighting up the fields so drear,
Praise the giver of the Springtime
    Who has sent them earth to cheer.

There's a murmur from the woodland,
    And I know its meaning well;

For the tender buds are growing,—
   Trees the gentle message tell.
In the pale green of the grass-blades,
   In the warmer winds, I hear:
" Bless the Giver of the Springtime
   Who has sent us earth to cheer."

Oh, the joy to read that message,
   With its wondrous grace and charm,
In the sky, soft bending o'er us,
   Like a mother's loving arm.
And my happy heart is singing,
   With the bluebirds, blithe and clear;
"Thank the Giver of the Springtime
   For his days of hope and cheer."

AT THE FAIR.

OH fair White City of the West !
   Oh, happy day and thought,
That led us on our raptured quest
   To see earth's wonders wrought !

The eyes are dazzled with the sheen
   Of beauty past compare ;
Oh, could my pen describe the scene
   That met my vision there !

Oh, could my lips in words portray
   The majesty of grace,
The ever varied, grand display,
   As vistas there we trace !

There Eastern worlds and Northern zones,—
   South, West, each other greet,
In grandest unison of tones,
   To make a world complete.

Jewels and gems of richest hue,
   And worth a monarch's throne.
Were there presented to our view ;
   But jewels not alone,—

The jewels of all industries,
   (The progress of the world)
As countless as the waves of seas,
   We there beheld impearled.

Whatever mind of man designed,
   Whatever womankind has wrought,
Yon fair White City hath enshrined—
   Rich gems of hand and thought.

The grand old masters we beheld,
   In Art's sublime domain ;
We gazed in wonder, awe-compelled,
   'Neath Painting's hallowed fane.

There Sculpture, genius-crowned appeared,
   In all its majesty ;
By time's own mighty hand endeared
   Through ages yet to be.

Oh, mighty wheel, with ceaseless whirl !
   Oh, kindred of the spheres !
As if from space it took its place,
   A comet through the years.

Oh, towers, whence we looked below
   Upon vast human throngs !
In every heart fond pleasure's glow,
   And grand thanksgiving songs.

Thanksgiving songs that all the earth
   Should there in friendship meet,
And, hand in hand, from every land
   America should greet.

Lo ! as we gazed upon that throng,
   From dazzling heights above,
Equality was still our song,
   And *Unity* and *Love.*

Queen City of the West, 'tis thine
   To call from every land
Its throngs, to worship at the shrine
   Of Freedom proud and grand.

Thy pageant lingers in our dreams,
   Shall live forevermore.
Thy fair White City fondly beams
   Our dazzled gaze before.

The tributes of the world to-day
   Are showered at thy feet,
And until time shall pass away,
   The ages thee shall greet.

One truth immortal gleams more bright
   Than countless treasures there,—
'Tis this, that *Liberty* and *Light*
   And *Freedom* crown the fair.

AUTUMN DAYS.

A VOICE from far-off hills
   Of sunlit amethyst;
The lisp of flashing rills
   By morning's ruby kissed;
The purple, garnet, gold,
   Of crisp leaves on the tree;—
   All things now say :
    " Where does she stray ?
Sweet summer, where is she?"

Bright flowers that gemmed her throne
 Fall from their settings fair;
The wind's sad monotone
 Voices the Year's despair.
Swift birds that follow her
 Have lost their warbled glee;
  With smile so gay,
  Where does she stay?
 Sweet Summer, where is she?

Her voice lives in our dreams;
 Her memories are bright,
Long treasured are her gleams,—
 Her visions of delight.
What though the dead leaves hide
 Her steps on lawn and lea?
  The heart shall say
  For many a day:
 "Sweet Summer, where is she?"

MUSING UPON THE DEATH OF A
BELOVED SON.

I.

DEAR little Georgie gone?
    No more to come.
First thoughts at break of dawn
    In this our home.

II.

No matter where we are
    His face we see—
Like a clear heavenly star
    He seems to be.

III.

For one sweet kiss from him
    My life I'd give,
For one more look at him
    No longer live.

IV.

Oh, he was bound to me
    By chords divine,
Strong as eternity,
    That boy of mine.

v.

Him, I can ne'er forget,
Though years should roll
E'en till life's sun is set,
Twined to my soul.

vi.

Dear Jesus thou alone
Canst give me peace,
Thy promises atone,
And grant release.

vii.

In Thee my trust is stayed,
Be this my joy,
When earthly joys shall fade
I'll meet my boy.

JESUS ONLY.

JESUS only ! Jesus only !
  Thou art all the world to me !
Fold me in thine arms of mercy,
  Let me, trusting lean on Thee !

Jesus only ! Jesus only !
  Keep temptation from my way,
I am weak but Thou art mighty;
  Be my rock, my staff, my stay.

Jesus only ! Jesus only !
  Hide from me all doubts and fears,
Heal my wounded, fainting spirit,
  Dry my sad and weary tears.

Jesus only ! Jesus only !
  This my safeguard ever be ;
Trusting in Thy tender kindness,
  Saviour, shield and shelter me !

Jesus only ! Jesus only !
  Be Thou near in life, in death.
I would praise Thee, Jesus, only,—
  Love Thee with my dying breath !

AFTER DARK.

HOW wondrously sweet is the light of day,
　　So clear and so sunny and fair ;
It scatters the gloomiest visions away,
　　And breaketh the chains of despair.

When darkness has folded his mantle around,
　　How often temptations lurk near ;
The vilest and cruelest deeds oft abound
　　To bring the heart many a tear.

The city, uncovered, at low tide is then,
　　The poisonous air reeks with sin ;
In many a hidden and horrible den
　　The reign of King Vice will begin.

The chance-made acquaintance upon the street
　　Means danger and misery near ;
The flattering smiles that may artfully greet
　　Should fill all who see them with fear.

They mean but a free pass to horrible death
　　On sin's whirling lightning express ;
Each station you pass, till life's weariest breath,
　　Your honor each hour growing less.

Oh, youth that safely at home should keep !
　　Nor roam through the darkness, at will ;
'Tis heaven ordained you these hours for sleep,
　　In quietude far from all ill.

My heart now goes out to you, earnest young boys,
　　'Twould shield you from every snare.
I watch you, full oft, in your innocent joys,
　　So far from the shadows of care.

I'd turn you forever from danger and woe,
　　From dark paths of sorrow and sin ;
And onward and upward I'd still bid you go
　　The highest of honors to win.

As still you press bravely to manhood's fair years,
　　Though temptations hover around,
May parents of yours never cause have for tears ;—
　　Their love,—be with thee ever bound.

Let home be a sacred and soul-hallowed spot,
　　The shelter from sin and from care ;
With loved ones anear that shall ne'er be forgot,
　　Thrice blest, with affection and prayer.

And, when life, with all that so puzzles us here,
　　Shall soar to its rest, as the lark,
Oh, may the fair dawning be radiant and clear
　　To greet every soul.—after dark !

WHERE THE WEARY ARE AT REST.

WHILE the purple shadows deepen 'round
　　my life so sad and lone,
And the cruel winds are beating o'er my path so
　　dreary grown,
I can hear a sweet voice calling, saying: "Cheer
　　up! bear the test,
And thou'lt wear a crown of glory where the weary
　　are at rest!"

Then begone all storm and darkness!—then away
　　all idle fears!
I am going to a city where there are no parting
　　tears.
He is waiting there to greet me,—the dear one I
　　love the best,—
Where the wicked cease from troubling, and the
　　weary are at rest.

May my footsteps never falter, as I journey day by
　　day,
Till I gain the golden portals whence all shadows
　　fly away.
Oh, the mansions of the Father, in those regions
　　of the blest,
Where the wicked cease from troubling, and the
　　weary are at rest!

85

Thus, while purple shadows deepen, oft I dream of
    realms afar,
And a little face shines on me, bright as evening's
    early star.
All my soul to go is longing, as a bird longs for its
    nest,
Up to yonder land eternal, where the weary are at
    rest.

THE FARMER'S CHRISTMAS GIFT.

(BALLAD.)

THE silver sound of sleigh bells tinkled, tinkled
    on the air;
The farmer sat beside the fire, his hale, old wife
    was there.
He looked upon the ruddy logs, and dreamed of
    days agone,—
Of happy Christmas eves of old when smiles upon
    him shone.

"Ah, wife," at last, he softly said, "in yonder
    blaze I see
The face of one who long ago was lost to you and
    me.
Of one who left the dear old farm, and left her
    parents' side;
Far better had it been for her if early she had
    died."

The weeping, trembling, poor old wife spake consolation sweet,
And silent tears coursed down their cheeks, while
 fell the snow and sleet;
The red logs crackled on the hearth, and seemed to
 whisper there
A message full of comfort to the bowed and wrinkled
 pair.

The farmer sees a happy child that whispers sweet
 good-night,
He holds her to his bosom with a father's fond
 delight;
Her stocking, in the chimney nook, is hung with
 childish glee;
'Tis Christmas Eve, and off to bed she scampers
 merrily.

Again, he sees a youthful pair who ask his blessing
 dear;
He speaks in anger, and his child departs in pride
 and fear.
A match, not of his seeking, calls a curse from out
 those lips,
And life upon that lonely farm then sinks to dark
 eclipse.

Alas! the anger long since died that made his days
 so drear;
"Oh, give me back my darling child!" he cried,
 while fell the tear;

"How could I thrust her from my heart?   Where
    lingers she to-night?
Perhaps in want, amid the city's far-off sin and
    blight."

Again that silver sound of sleigh bells.   Hark !
    no more 'tis heard !
Then footsteps coming to the porch, with just one
    joyful word.
That word was "Home !"   The farmer and his
    wife are at the door,—
It opens, all their happiness to give them back
    once more.

The flame leaps brighter on the hearth as if with
    hearty glee.
"Thank God, my darling daughter, he has sent
    you back to me !
Your husband?   Oh, forgive the words I spoke so
    long ago !
'Twas ill to speak so harshly, and repentance came
    not slow.

"The merriest of Christmas Eves for many a year
    is mine.
Ah ! dear old wife, your eyes with sweetest happi-
    ness may shine !
The wind without may fiercely blow, the snow may
    wildly drift,
But what care we, for God has sent to us our
    Christmas gift."

TO THE SUN.

OH, dawning sun, how beautiful,
  How wondrous are thy beams !
All nature sinks to welcome thee,
  A Paradise earth seems.

When I behold thy quickening power,
  And comprehend thy worth,
I gaze upon thy rays with awe,
  And hushed is joy and mirth.

Ah ! well I know how weak we are,--
  God's children here below ;
But thou hast gifts for everyone
  In thy awakening glow.

How infinite thy matchless strength,
  How glorious thy power ;
God's poem written in the sky
  At dawn, at twilight hour.

Thy golden, purple, crimson hues,
  At sunset, seem to be
The pathway leading out of Time
  To blest Eternity.

PARTED.

WHERE shall our next meeting be?
On the land, or on the sea?
Forest, meadow, hill or grove;
Which shall view our kiss of love?

Some day, after all our pain,
I must clasp thee once again;
Some day, whether far or near,
I shall see that face so dear.

Mutual faith and trust can bridge
Over Time's tempestuous ridge;
Whether lives be rich or poor,
Truest love will e'er endure.

Hasten! kiss my lips once more,
As thou didst in days of yore!
Fold me in those arms again!
Must my longing be in vain?

Heart of mine, wait patiently
Till thy loved shall come to thee;
Trusting, watching, waiting, now,
With Hope's star upon thy brow.

Joys of life I may possess,
And with treasures Time may bless,—
Still life's void can not be filled,
Till my longing heart be stilled.

With thy presence, pure and sweet,
Which my spirit longs to greet,
Answer, "some day I shall come
Never from thy side to roam."

DECORATION DAY.

(1891.)

ANOTHER year has rolled around,
   And brought its gift of flowers
To lay above each honored mound
   Of these dear dead of ours.

Another year—a thousand years
   Can lessen not the love
That watches o'er these graves with tears,
   As angels watch above !

Another year has borne away
   Two gallant hearts and bold;
Their deathless names, in proud array,
   See ! on Fame's page enscrolled.

Our gallant *Porter*, pure as dew
    In knightly loyalty ;
Our hero, *Sherman*, spotless, true,
    Has halted at the Sea.

These join the ranks of noble dead
    Whose graves to us are dear;
Be sweetest bloom above them spread
    With each returning year.

O, young hearts, keep with faithful trust
    The memory of our brave !
O, nation, honor still the dust
    Of those who died to save !

Bring flowers—the red, the white, the blue,
    To tell in language plain
They gave not up those lives so true
    Nor fought nor bled in vain.

Comrades in many a storied fray,
    Tread softly where they lie ;
Their love is in all hearts to-day,
    Their fame shall never die.

"REMEMBER ME!"

"REMEMBER me!" sweetly it fell from thy
        lips;
Again I can hear it, though death's dark eclipse
Has hidden thy face from mortality's view,
Oh, friend ever loving and gentle and true!

"I would not live alway," I hear thee still say,
Where storm after storm rises dark o'er the way!
Now gone is the tempest for thee evermore,
And calm is thine home, on yon peace-hallowed
    shore.

How strangely those words now awake in the heart;
They seem of thy spirit and being a part:
I can not forget them, they bring to me, now,
Thy dear patient face, and thy smile-lighted brow.

Not *here* to live alway!—but, in God's bright land,
To sing with the angels in harmony grand!
Thou still art remembered, dear heart, till we meet,
For friendship clasps ever thy memory sweet.

A CITY INCIDENT.

NIGHT o'er the city, dark and chill;
  The winds go shrieking by,
Like demons, bent on direst ill,
  They toss the snow-drifts high.
The weary toiler's work is o'er,
  And on, with hastening feet,
He seeks his welcome home once more
  His loved ones there to greet.

But louder than the raging blast
  Those sounds of wildest din,
From where yon lurid light is cast,—
  The haunts of woe and sin.
And fiercer than the storm without,
  The raging passions there,—
The curses deep, the maniac shout,
  That herald dark despair.

" Fill high the bowl ! drink deep to-night !"
  Cries one, "away with thought !"
See how the liquor sparkles bright,
  It brings the joys we sought.
Again the maudlin laugh rings on;
  The glasses gaily clink;
A siren's tune to lure each one
  Towards Ruin's yawning brink.

What unseen specters hover there,
   Above that flame-fed crowd;
A dying mother, and her prayer,
   A father, sorrow-bowed.
A wife and children, crouched in fear,
   While blows are falling fast;
The shadow of a gallows near,
   A pauper's grave, at last.

Still howls the storm; the lights descend;
   The revelers depart;
What is it, ere his footsteps wend,
   One clasps unto his heart?
A little bundle, snowy white,
   That lies beside the door:
"Oh God! my child!" in wild affright
   A father mutters o'er.

" I came to bring you home, papa,
   But I was turned away;
And I have walked so very far,
   I thought for you I'd stay.
I'm glad you're here; I feel such pain:"
   No more those white lips said;
The father kissed his child again,
   The little one was dead.

" Speak! Speak! my darling, speak to me!
   Oh, wretched fool was I!
The cause of all this misery—
   I led you here to die."

'Out of the heartless, maudlin crowd,
    He hastened with his child,
And o'er the icy burden bowed
    In grief and anguish wild.

*   *   *   *   *

Oh, myriad voices of despair !
    Oh, hearts that broken lie !
Oh, souls oppressed with endless care !
    The curse of Drink must die.
By all on earth we love the best,
    We'll work, heart, soul and hand,
With energy that knows no rest,
    To sweep Rum from our land !

A KISS IN DREAMS.

OH, rapturous gladness and exquisite bliss !
    What hope o'er my way fondly beams;
A world of affection may dwell in a kiss,—
    You kissed me last night in my dreams.

Blest moment supreme, and a foretaste of Heaven !
    Your spirit was hovering near,
No greater delight unto mortals is given
    Than shone in your glances so dear.

The shadows and storms of my life passed away,
  I lived in the days that had flown;
Sweet love o'er my being held infinite sway,
  And once again you were my own.

I woke from my vision, beholding you gone,
  And dull grew life's radiant beams;
Oh, darling, in twilight or midnight or dawn,
  Come, kiss me again in my dreams!

CHRISTMAS.

CHIME on, oh, merry Christmas bells!
  Your tuneful, glad accord,
With sweetest music, softly tells
  Of Christ, our risen Lord.
When we recall that lowly birth,
  In cradled manger lone,
We wonder not at praise and mirth,
  All hail, thou sacred morn!

For since thy dawn "Peace and good will"
  On earth have been impearled,
For those believing, He is still
  The Saviour of the world.
Then ring out, bells! Your silver song
  Soothes many a weary way;
Glorias and anthems well belong
  To thee, glad Christmas day!

Venite Adoremus sing
  With glad acclaim to-day !
Let hallelujahs loudly ring
  This hallowed Christmas day.
And, while the carol riseth now,
  In praise of His dear name,
Our hearts in adoration bow
  Since He our King became.

Oh, children, what a morn to you,
  As trouping down the stairs,
With eyes of hope, like sparkling dew,
  Ye charm away our cares.
But those whose arms are empty now,
  How wearisome life's hours !
While on this once glad day ye bow
  Over a grave's dead flowers.

Oh, folded hands and loving eyes
  Safe in that upper fold !—
Rejoicing in yon paradise,
  In streets of shining gold.
Your sweet good-by we'll ne'er forget;
  Ye lead us all the way;
For promised hope abideth yet
  On this dear Christmas day.

Oh, may we ever look above
  To yonder white-robed choir !
May we, by their dear, sacred love,
  Be guided on still higher.

Hosannas in excelsis sing !
　Bring offerings glad to-day,
For unto Him, our chosen King,
　We chant our Christmas lay.

CAROL, CHILDREN, CAROL !

CAROL on this blessèd morn
　　How the Prince of Peace was born,
In the manger all forlorn.
　　　　Carol, children, carol !

CHORUS.

Hark ! the angels' song again
Sounding over hill and glen:
" Peace on earth, good will to men ! "
　　　　Carol, children, carol !

Carol how the star, so bright,
Led the wise men through the night,
To the Babe,—oh, wondrous sight !
　　　　Carol, children, carol !

Carol how upon the plain
Shepherds heard the heav'nly strain,—
Never shall its glory wane.
　　　　Carol, children, carol !

Carol, carol, far and near,
Glory to our Saviour dear !
On this morn of all the year,—
            Carol, children, carol !

GOLDEN LINKS.

OH, the golden link that binds me
        To yonder home so blest,
Where my darling one is waiting
    To welcome me to rest !

He is waiting with the Saviour,
    And, when my toil's complete,
He is the link that holds me,—
    A gem at Jesus' feet.

Oh, the past, the present, future,
    Have radiance untold,
While that bright link still binds me
    To streets of precious gold !

Let me hallow this, God's token,
    Through life my endless joy,—
This link 'twixt me and Heaven,—
    My darling, angel boy !

MIDWINTER WOODS.

A CAVE where wizard Winter dwells,—
   These dim, white solitudes o'erhung
With weird stalactites, in wide cells,
   High vaulted. Where sweet birds have sung,
No sound is heard but the gride of wind-swept
     boughs above, below,
And the snap of icicles that shrill along the crusted
     snow,
         In these midwinter woods.

Naught here betokens life, save prints,
   Soft tinted, of the rabbit's tread;
No whisper, in the air, that hints
   Of milder hours. The brooklet's bed
That winds, a silver snake, is lost in distant,
     billowy drifts,
And not one golden ray glints through the cheer-
     less, blackened rifts
         Of these midwinter woods.

O, ashen sky that bodes full long
   But dearth and storm and dreary days !
But hark ! a chicadee's blithe song,
   Like smitten silver, haunts these ways !

O, bird of clearer faith than mine, and keener eyes
      to see,
Beneath the mantle of the snow, the blossoms
      soon to be
                In these midwinter woods.

DOWN WHERE THE MOHAWK GLIDETH.

DOWN where the Mohawk glideth
    To meet the deep blue sea,
A maiden dwells, 'mid lily bells,
  And she is all this world to me.
Her dark blue eyes are beaming
  With lovelight all the day;
And oh ! her words, like songs of meadow birds
  Make sweet life's weary way !

Her step is gentle as the rippling stream.
Her smile is lovely as the starry beam.
There she waits me just as the daylight is fading to
    eve;
Sweetest darling, eyes so entrancing and roguishly
    glancing
While loving dreams the glad moments ever so
    gracefully weave
Down where the stream flows like a dream
Through the Mohawk's vale !

Down where the Mohawk glideth
So peacefully along,
And to the flowers in golden hours,
Repeats its glad and tuneful song.
I told love's tender story
Forever fond and true,
And sweet the smile beamed on me all the while
From out her eyes of blue.

Down where the Mohawk glideth
  I won her loving heart !
And from her side, whate'er betide,
  I never shall in life depart.
Our home will be all sunshine
  Each dawn with love we'll hail ;
And rapture fair shall ever bless us there
  In our sweet Mohawk vale.

DREAMS.

I.

WHAT dreams, by night, my fancies weave,
    When sleep o'ertakes mine eyes!
Oh, do they come to cheer or grieve?
    Come they from earth or skies?

How oft I see those whom I knew
    In school days, long ago,
What forms that now are hid from view,
    Resting from storms and woe.

Can it be true they come again
    To bless and aid us here?
To bid us fly from sin and pain,
    To banish haunting fear?

To tell us that earth is not all,
    That there's another life!
Oh, listen to the tones that fall
    To calm our daily strife!

I can not fathom all my dreams;
    But this I feel and know:
The soul still lives in sunlit gleams
    When lies this body low.

II.

Why do I dream of my loved boy so much,
  From the close of the day till the dawn?
Why do I feel his dear hands as they touch,
  And awake, but to know he is gone?

Why do I rock him to sleep in my chair,
  Pressing close to my heart his dear head?
Why do I smooth my hand over his hair,
  When they tell me that Georgie is dead?

I will not believe them, it can not be true,
  For he lives in a glorious sphere;
His eyes still are beaming with Heaven's own blue,
  And he comes in my dreams but to cheer.

Soon I shall seek him, with angels to sing,
  Where I'll press him to my aching heart.
Soon he will come the blest message to bring
  That we never in Heaven shall part.

III.

In dreams, a hand beckoned me yonder,
  Through the clouds, so heavenly fair;
Three times I saw it, and I wonder
  What the message it doth bear.

Oh, am I through with earthly sorrow,
  And through with burdens hard to bear?
Doth it portend to me no morrow,
  An end to every weary care?

'Twould be no cross, oh, hand celestial,
　To soar away where thou dost dwell !
To leave this dwelling place terrestrial,
　If that's the message thou dost tell.

For there has gone my heart's fond treasure,
　And here I'm striving to prepare,
That when this earthly life I measure
　I may obtain an entrance there.

Yes; fairest hopes of mine have perished;
　And sered the flowers within my heart.
The fondest ties I here have cherished
　Were rudely sundered wide apart.

Dost herald, then, some new awaking ?
　Ethereal stranger, to me speak !
Explain the signs that thou art making,
　And whom it is that thou dost seek.

What message hast thou, Heavenly stranger
　That thou hast beckoned me, at night ?
Perhaps thou warnest me of danger,
　Oh, mystic hand so weirdly white !

Oh, may I heed thy silent calling !
　My dearest hopes on Heaven are built;
Sad heart, when deathly gloom is falling,
　Thy song be " Saviour, as Thou wilt."

"SHE IS MY QUEEN ALONE!"

SHE is my gem, my little treasure,
　　Yes she is mine and mine alone !
Her boundless love, oh who could measure?
　　Who would not worship at her throne ?
She drives away all gloom and sorrow,
　　And makes earth seem a paradise;
She grows more dear to me each morrow,
　　While fondly I look in her bright eyes.

CHORUS:

　　She's mine !　Yes, mine !
　　　　My love will last forever !
　　　　　So neat, so sweet,
　　This little dimpled darling of my life.
　　　　　We'll meet, and greet,
　　　　And parted shall be never;
　　　She is my queen of love,
　　　　As true as stars above,
　And soon she will be my happy wife.

Bright is her smile where joy reposes
　　Long, long ago I won her heart ;
Her cheeks are red as summer roses,
　　Her smile is far beyond all art.

I'd freely give the pearls of ocean
    One gentle smile of hers to own;
She holds my heart's supreme devotion,
    My darling !   She is my queen alone.

A RAINY DAY.

DARK with rain the clouds may be,
    And a mist drape all with gloom;
Sad thy life may seem to thee,
    O'erpressed with sense of doom;
Yet, beyond the clouds is light.—
    There is sunshine full of cheer ;
The passing shadows only blight
    To make God's sun more clear.

Hopeless heart, no more repine;
    Let thy vision pierce the gloom.
Joy and rest may still be thine;
    Life's roses still shall bloom.
Lift thy burdens once again,
    With a faith and trust secure.
Beyond the shadow and the pain
    His love doth still endure.

MUSIC.

OH, music, dear comrade, through many long
       years,
As time glided by you have banished my fears,
While onward and upward you guide me along,
My heart is o'erflowing with jubilant song.

Forget you? Ah, no! you are far, far too dear;
Unto my sad life you have brought welcome cheer.
How fondly I cherish you, music, fair art,
You strike the sweet chords that are deep in my
      heart.

Then into my bosom, dear music, oh, steal;
Charm all that is darksome in life, and unreal.
Your cadences sing me, so softly and low,
That tempests and sorrows may far from me go.

And when the last note shall be struck by my hand,
And in earth's grand chorus no longer I stand,
Oh, be it my mission in Heaven to play,
Before the white throne, in angelic array!

TO A RAINBOW.

THOU bow of promise, welcome, bright,
   With all thy vernal hue,
With cheerfulness we watch thy light
   That glads the year so new.
For thou dost come in joyous May,
   A promise to the earth
That summer shall not long delay,
   That gone is winter's dearth.

I welcome thee, sweet bow of hope
   Shine o'er us evermore.
Dear friends, beyond our vision's scope,
   Thou'rt fondly bending o'er.
Thou givest joy with each bright ray,
   Each hue hath power divine;
How could the heart e'er go astray
   From promises of thine.

Though seldom is thy advent here,
   Thy loveliness hath power
To quell the sad and lonely fear,
   And bid us hope each hour.
For know we not God's promise sure,
   Through ages, is the same?
Our faith in Him must still endure,
   For thou dost breathe His name.

LOVELY JUNE.

AIR: "HOME AGAIN."

LOVELY June! Lovely June!
  Sweet the hours you bring;
We long to see your smiling face,
  And hear your warblers sing.
Your blushing rose, your lily fair,
  Have crowned our earth with joy;
And oh, our mem'ries bright of you
  No winter can destroy.

Lovely June! &c.

Lovely June! Lovely June!
  Keep within our hearts;
For every charm that comes with you
  Sweet happiness imparts.
Within our grange, oh, whisper sweet
  Your harmonies divine!
And round each sister's gentle heart
  Your garlands still entwine.

Lovely June! &c.

JOHNSTOWN FLOOD.

THE dewy morn was fair and bright,
  That peaceful summer's day;
The rising sun, with golden light,
  Smiled, beaming, on its way.
The birds were singing merrily,
  Sweet flowers shed perfume;
The city seemed in peace to be,
  None feared impending doom.

Bedecked in wedding robes, a bride
  Before the altar stands;
The groom awaiting, by her side,
  The priest to join their hands.
The wedding march had just been played,
  The bridal party bow;
A wreath of flowers now is laid
  Upon her youthful brow.

Another scene, not far from there:
  We mark a funeral shroud;
We list the solemn uttered prayer
  Ascending unto God.
We see the mourners drawing near
  To take their last farewell;
When suddenly a cry we hear
  Ring like a requiem knell.

A horseman, on his steed of bay,
    Flies, shouting, o'er the vale:
"Make haste! run for your lives! away!"
    He shrieks with echoing wail.
Madly, and with stupendous sway,
    Gigantic in its power,
The water swept both sad and gay,
    The shroud and bridal bower.

Deep horror filled the hearts of all!
    Gone was the humble roof;
Spire, mansion, totter to their fall,
    Death now stands not aloof,
But rides upon the current wild
    To shatter and destroy.
Oh, where has flown the scene so mild
    In homes of peace and joy?

A child, raft-swept upon the wave,
    Now pleads, with pallid brow:
"You told me God would always save,—
    Oh, mamma, will he now?"
Another group, in calm despair,
    Awaiting death we see,
Kneeling together, singing there:
    "Nearer my God to Thee!"

And thou, brave rider and thy steed
    Dead at thy duty's post!
Thy life a ransom given indeed,
    Worthy the martyred host.

No truer heart had ever crossed
   O'er blood-red fields of fray;
No braver life was ever lost
   Than thine, that fatal day.

Ah ! sweet to die that we may save !
   God's hero sent to earth !
Long in our hearts shall live the brave
   Enshrined in deathless worth.
Seek not the ranks of war afar
   For bravery alone;
'Tis where the humble loyal are,
   The silent and unknown.

Oh, gallant hero, sweetly sleep !
   Fearless, thou sought to save
Life from the raging waters deep.
   Rest, heart so truly brave !
And may the time be very near
   When through that vale again
The bells shall ring out peace and cheer,
   And gladness long shall reign.

SUMMER-TIME.

OH, we are companions this golden day,—
　　The birds and the bees and the soft blue sky,
The lilies, the brook with its roundelay,
　　The rocks and the grass, the leaves and I.
I live in their gladness; and, hour by hour,
　　We speak to each other a language sweet.
　　　　　　Ah ! could I unfold
　　　　　　The joy is told,
　　What rapture of song would my lips repeat
　　　　　　　　　Of summer-time !

Deep-aureoled sunset,—the birds wing home
　　With new, garnered joy for to-morrow's praise;
The sky gathers orbs in its purple dome;
　　The brook to the sea bears pleasant lays;
The bees have their largess, each flower-cup its
　　　　　　pearl;
　　And I, as I wander my path along,
　　　　　　Take with me away
　　　　　　New joy to-day,—
　　New life,—and this breath of an idle song
　　　　　　　　　Of summer-time !

THE MISSION OF FLOWERS.

OH, the beautiful mission of flowers,—
   The gems of the earth are they;
Uplifting the loneliest hours
   That meet us from day to day.
There is joy in their fragrance rare,
   And hope in their lustre clear;
And friendship and beauty fair
   In summer's companions dear.

To the sick and the weary they bring
   A joy that is all untold;
Life's winter is turned to spring,
   Its dross unto burnished gold.
In their petals the morning sun
   Forever in glory beams;
And ever till life is done
   Are memory's fadeless gleams.

There are visions that never decay
   Of those who have gone before.
They bring us, o'er life's dark way,
   The kisses we know no more.
Though the hand is now cold that gave,
   Ah ! who of us can forget
The love that beyond the grave
   Lives on in some violet.

Oh, the beautiful mission of flowers
    Earth-sent by the Lord above,
To teach us in weariest hours
    A lesson of light and love.
There is joy, in each daisy fair
    That stars every field and dell;
And the humblest flower everywhere
    Has a message from God to tell.

OUR GRANGE.

AIR: "RED, WHITE AND BLUE."

OUR Grange be the theme of our chorus,
    Its influence spreading afar,
And bright be the pathway before us
    While truth guides us on like a star.
No idle dissensions o'ercloud us,
    But sweetest devotion inspire;
May selfishness never enshroud us,—
    Our motto be "Higher still Higher!"

Our Grange be the theme of our song,
May gladness its mission prolong;
Oh, thus on each festal day ever,
Our Grange be the theme of our song!

Our Grange,—'tis the heart's deep devotion,
   'Tis there we may lovingly meet;
Its sway rules from ocean to ocean,
   Oh, still keep its unity sweet!
Its bright festal days keep we ever
   And unto its teachings be true;
For it be each heart's best endeavor,
   While seasons their bounty renew.

Our Grange be the theme, &c.

A SUMMER'S DAY.

OH, breath of the summer, how sweet unto
        me!
Some token of love in each floweret I see,—
Some new hope is wakened, by Heaven, in the
    heart
Of those who are thoughtfully bearing life's part.

By blue of old ocean, as raptured I stand,
I gaze on the work of His almighty hand;
And the wild sparkling waves, as in beauty they
    leap,
Give voice to His majesty wondrous and deep.

In each silent blossom, so fragrant and fair,
Are tributes of love that the Father placed there.
Shall I not then praise Him, and, jubilant sing,
In this tiny song of the summer I bring?

ALL HAIL OUR QUEEN.

AIR: "AMERICA."

ALL hail our radiant queen !
　　From hills and meadows green
　　　We gather here.
With heart and soul elate,
We own thy sway so great,
And for thy message wait
　　　From year to year.

Our queen superb art thou !
With homage do we bow
　　　Before thy throne.
Thy teaching to each heart,
From day to day impart,
For loveliness thou art
　　　From zone to zone.

Beauty and grace divine,—
These symbols fair are thine,
　　　And faith and love.
To Him who sent this day,
Oh, give our thanks alway !
All hearts Thy will obey,
　　　Great God above.

119

FLORA DAY.

WE hail thee, lovely Day of flowers !
    Oh, joy again to meet,
Amid the gems from Nature's bowers,
    Of fragrance rare and sweet !
Oh, Flora, Queen of radiant reign !
    Our Grange, with royalty,
Thou hast in gladness wreathed again
    And summer's greenery.

We welcome thee,—thy subjects true,
    With ardor and delight.
Crowned with thy garlands fresh with dew,
    Oh, boon unto our sight !
Thy throne a bank of roses fair,
    Thy scepter lilies twined,
Thy realm the summer everywhere,
    In every heart enshrined.

We give our hearts to thee this day,
    For peace and love abound;
There's gladness in thy colors gay,
    With song thy life is crowned.
Oh, use thy influence so bright
    Where'er thy votaries meet !
Make Flora Day a dear delight,
    A symbol pure and sweet.

A BIRD'S SONG.

I.

WHILE bobolinks are piping clear,
    And robins flute all day;
While blackbirds in the glades we hear,
    And daisies light the way;
A pensive voice, from nook remote,
Gives utterance to one sad note:
        " Phœbe !   Phœbe ! "

II.

It mocks the witchery of Spring,
    The glory of the leaves,
While fragrant blossoms lightly cling,—
    This tiny voice that grieves.
Oh, bird that pleads so plaintively,
Has thy fond nest-mate gone from thee?
        " Phœbe !   Phœbe ! "

ABSENCE.

THOUGH Southern skies are o'er thee, dear,
   Where sweet magnolias grow,
The North, without thee, seems more drear, —
   Darker than thou canst know.

While Winter's mine, with snow and gloom,
   Thine is the gentle May;
Soon orange trees will be in bloom,
   And roses bright and gay.

Could I take wings, I'd fly, dear heart,
   To clasp thee by the hand, —
I'd meet thee there, from all, apart,
   In thy fair sunny land.

Oh, sweet our meeting then would be !
   But, love, I'll murmur not,
Though I am far, so far from thee,
   If I am ne'er forgot.

OLD AGE.

A TREASURE of wisdom hath ripe old age,
  And what knowledge it can impart,—
Experience written on Life's clear page,
  To instruct and improve the heart.
We read where a Monarch once bowed his head
  To a shepherd who roamed the hills;
And a sweet benediction of light was shed
  O'er his Life with its joys and ills !

E'en now, oft the blessings of dear, old sires
  Bring us rest, as we trod Life's way;
Experience, ripened as if through fires,
  Points a path to us, day by day.
Yea, Jacob did bless an anointed King,
  In the centuries long ago !
And all honor and glory did proudly cling
  To the blessing he did bestow.

Oh, words of the aged ne'er cast aside,
  But with meekness receive and heed !
How precious are they to a Youth untried,
  How they answer the spirit's need !
With reverence, then, we should bow the knee
  To the old, when they counsel give;
For the perils beyond us they clearly see,
  They can teach us the way to live !

Oh, the wonderful boon for a heart to beat
    Through its journey of four-score years !—
Still patiently treading the dust and heat,
    And enduring the cares and tears !
Then scorn not the lesson they would impart,
    For to Youth 'tis a precious gain;
And 'twill lighten the burden where'er thou art,
    And 'twill turn thee from paths of pain.

Protect thou the aged with constant love,
    For they linger not with us long !
Their Father is waiting for them above,
    They are waiting, to sing His song !
Their sweet benediction be ever ours,
    While so gently they linger here;
O'er their pathway still scatter the sweetest flowers,
    As the down hill of Life we cheer !

SO TIRED.

WHEN Night calls weary ones to rest,
　　My thoughts fly far away ;
I think of noble hearts, worn out,
　　With cares and toils of day.
Oh, ye, o'erburdened with your grief !
　　Oh, ye, oppressed with care !
Rest now your faith on Him who said :
　　" All sorrows I will bear."

My thoughts go back, on dove-like wings,
　　To Ages long ago,
When David, King of Israel,
　　Grew tired through grief and woe ;
When sad of soul he sat him down,
　　His Kingly harp in hand,
Remembering how, a shepherd lad,
　　He sang of that blest Land.

" My rod and staff they comfort me,
　　My Shepherd's voice sustains ;
He leadeth me, He strengtheneth me,
　　To bear earth's grief and pain !"
Though we're not Kings, yet everyone
　　Has his or her small realm ;
We all need help from this dear Friend
　　To guide our vessel's helm.

The rich, the poor, complain alike—
    " We're tired to death " they say ;
No matter what their lot may be,
    They worry all the day.
Down, wolf of Drink !—to vex and fret :
    Down, worry, vice and woe !
Come, rod and staff, to comfort all,
    And peace and love bestow.

Oh, Man of Nazareth, I believe
    In Thy Life, Death and Power !
Thy Word,—it rests and heals me now,
    I grasp its truth each hour.
It is my staff, it helps to cheer,
    It calms my anguish here ;
'Twill aid me surely, when I die,
    To know my Lord is near.

A SPRING FANCY.

ROBIN HOOD and his merry men,
Garbed in green, have come again !
Out with the bluebird's fluted song,
While buds, like bees, the branches throng.

Friar bold who heads the clan,
Winsome, sweet maid Marian,
Little John, and the archers near,
Glance in the morning breezy, clear.

Over hill and dale they throng,
Green plumes twinkling, mirth and song ;
Merry men all, and merry lass,
Mimicked in these blades of grass.

THE BALM OF KINDNESS.

OH, the rankling, the bitter and unkind word!
    How cruelly poignant its sting!
The heart from its depths is with anguish stirred
    When we hear its metallic ring.

When we're leaving our home, full of hope so
      bright,
    At morning, at noontide, or eve,
It darkens our path, like the dreariest night,
    While with torturing thoughts we grieve.

How it robs all our lives of their music and joy, —
    Embitters our sunniest hope!
Unwelcome it falls, but to bring annoy,
    While in anguish our spirits grope.

But oh, when it comes from a friend we love,
    Its dart then we doubly feel!
It falls, like a thunderbolt from above,
    Or a blade of the keenest steel.

Ah! it pierces the deeps of our inmost soul,
    And rankles with pitiless pain!
It would make, e'en of Heaven, perdition's goal!
    Stamp an Angel with deadly stain.

But oh, ye kind words, what a joy ye bring !
    What happiness, sunlight and bliss !
Ye make earth around us rejoice and sing,
    Who your wonderful balm would miss ?

Your breath is a joy to the wounded heart,
    When darkest of clouds hover o'er;
Ye lead us to choose that better part
    That will guide us to yon bright shore.

And when the glad sunshine of hope beams bright,
    And skies are all tranquil and clear,
Our hearts will retain their youthful light,
    If no unkindly words we hear.

And when, too, old age creeps upon Life's way
    With winds of the Winter so drear,
Then kind words illume with their gladsome ray
    All the gloom of our pathway here.

Ah, yes,—when we cross the brighter shore,
    And enter those mansions so pure,
Kind words from our Saviour will welcome us o'er
    Unto joys that will e'er endure !

FRIENDSHIP.

'TIS sweet to think of friends we love,
 When doubt and gloom hang o'er ;
Our minds in Fancy bright will rove
 To see their smiles once more.

Their faith so true, their aid and cheer,
 To us are golden rays,
Which lull to rest each weary fear
 Thro' Life's enshrouded days.

Methinks 'tis Heaven that gives us friends
 In every trying hour ;
To teach us that God's love extends
 Where darkest tempests lower.

Oh, let's be worthy of their love,—
 Their sympathy so sweet ;
Their messages are from above,
 With joy our hearts they greet.

Tho' troubles fall, and weary care
 May cast its shadows 'round,
'Tis happiness a friend to share
 And be in friendship bound.

All honor to the tried and true !
  They're ours, thro' pain and joy ;
Tho' they be numbered with the few,
  They're gold, without alloy !

What fickle friendships, once so dear,
  Have drifted far away.
We loved them well when they were near,
  They blest us for a day.

Beware of friends, only in name !
  When we have lost a friend,
We realize our love was vain,
  While sadly on we wend.

But there's a Friend will ne'er forsake
  Tho' grief and gloom be ours !
He steadfast is till dawn shall break,
  And sunlight gilds the showers.

If we're in care, He's at our side ;
  He's with us, when we weep ;
Tho' disappointments may betide,
  The Saviour watch doth keep.

He ever to His friends is true.
  Oh, follow where He trod !
His loving precepts still pursue,
  They lead to Heaven and God !

SNOWDROPS.

IN a flurry the snow-flakes fluttered down,
　　From a sudden cloud o'erhead ;
　　　　And the earth seemed new,
　　　　As they near it drew :
　　" Were strangers here," they said.

For the wand of the Spring hath touched the vales,
　　And the sod no longer slept ;
　　　　The brooks leaped out,
　　　　With a silvery shout,
　　And the grass blades upward crept.

Now the sunshine had only played " bo-peep :"
　　" I will catch these flakes," it said,
　　　　For I mark a grace
　　　　" On each pretty face ;
　　So my golden net I'll spread !"

Then it wove for them dresses of white and green,
　　And, one morning, breezy fair,
　　　　All the lonely side
　　　　Of a mountain wide
　　Lighted up with the snowdrops there !

EASTER.

WHY seek the living midst the dead?
    Be sure they are not there!
Why sadly, softly dost thou tread,
    And scatter flow'rets fair?
This Easter morn proclaims they live!
    This ground they never trod;
On Judgement Day behold! they give
    New bodies to this sod!

Oh, theme so grand we cannot grasp
    Nor fathom its bright ray!
We feel the thrill,—wait for the clasp
    Of Resurrection Day.
Glad heart of mine, dost thou not feel
    That this calm, hallowed hour
Is now the signet and the seal
    Of promised Life and power?

Though tasks remain unfinished here,
    In that Eternal Land
They shall survive,—shall reappear,
    If noble, true and grand!
Yes, all will then employment find
    If they with truth and love
And meekness discipline the mind:
    For them God's work above.

To know that Jesus rose again,
    Death loses half its sting !
Our fears it calms, it quells our pain,
    With thankful hearts we sing.
Oh, will the Angels then appear,
    And roll the stone away !
To you, to me, will they draw near
    On Resurrection Day?

God grant alone we may not be ;
    But with those spirits bright
May we be cheered eternally,
    And led to Life and Light.
We'll ride on chariot-clouds, we know,
    As Christ did long before;
Now buried in His likeness,—Lo !
    We rise, we breathe, we soar !

Bright Easter ! while we celebrate,
    Hark ! Herald-angels sing !
We know our loved ones there await,
    And hallelujahs sing.
Thus praying, through His only Son,
    God will direct our way,
We breathe aloud " Thy will be done,"
    And praise this Easter Day !

REST.

"There remaineth a rest for the people of God."

UNTO you there remaineth a rest,
    A rest, for the people of God.
Oh, let this be Life's richest bequest,
    Till all of Life's journey be trod !

Blessed Hope, sweetest boon unto me.
    You come, like a mild, healing balm ;
Our weary souls then shall be free,
    And heart-storms be lulled to a calm.

Here we struggle along through Life's care,
    Still striving to bear all its ills ;
Take courage ! we here but prepare
    For Rest, which the Saviour fulfills.

For an earnest of this blissful rest
    Our spirit can feel even now,
We must choose the fair path which is best,
    With dauntless and God-fearing brow.

Then all glory and praises be given
    Unto our Redeemer this day !
He hath kept, for the hearts that have striven,
    A rest that shall ne'er fade away.

A MOTHER'S LOSS.

(J. HARRY ALDRICH.)

MY absent boy ! My absent boy !
    This heart is aching now;
Life is for me a path of care,
    And throbs my anguished brow.
Thy bounding step I hear no more,
    I miss thy cheerful face;
The zest of Life, for me, is o'er,
    I long for thy embrace.

I see thy lone and vacant chair,
    And wonder, lingering near,
How long before I'll meet thee *there*,
    Thy gentle voice to hear.
Sometimes, when twilight's holy hour
    Steals o'er our joyless home,
I hear a voice,—some unseen power
    Says: "Mother, back I've come !"

Then rapture fills my heart once more !
    Sweet music fills the air !
I wake to find the bright dream o'er,
    And utter this fond prayer,—

That when Life's weary path is trod,
  In yonder realms of joy,
Within the mansions of my God
  I'll meet my absent boy.

EASTER-TIME.

AH ! not alone, in symbols bright,
    Let fonted lilies speak
Of Him, the way, the truth, the light,
  The lowly, meek.
Nor bells alone, to bending blue,
  Echo. with joyful breath,
The endless story, ever new,
  Of conquered Death.
But, pilgrim soul, where'er thou art,
  Hear Faith's clear, wakening chime,
And, with Hope's lilies in thy heart,
  Keep Easter-time !

THE WONDERFUL WHISPER.

WHAT volumes God whispers to the soul,
 Yea, listen and heed them well!
They come unto us, while the ages roll,
 Their warnings of love to tell.

Oh, hath He not said: " Friend, go in peace!
 Thy sins are forgiven thee?"
Uplifting the burden, and giving release:
 " I was once blind, now I see!"

Likewise, " My peace I give unto thee."
 Oh, not as the world doth give,—
It gives to the many, also to the few;
 But God's gift for aye shall live.

Oh, the clasp of a true, true Christian's hand!
 It cheereth Life's lonely way;
It leadeth us out of the weary night
 To beautiful dawn of day.

We must not wish Him to speak too loud;
 He can thunder in trumpet tones,
Or whisper e'en in the moving cloud,
 Or in rocks and rills and stones.

One Hour With Thee.

One hour with Thee, O dearest Jesus,
  In silence at Thy feet,
One hour of rest, of joy, of bliss,
  My God, My God how sweet:
To kneel before Thy earthly throne
  And gaze upon thee here,
To be one hour with thee alone,
  And oh to be so near.

What can I do? What can I say?
  How praise, how thank, how love,
What fitting homage can I pay?
  O, angels from above.
Lend me your voices for one hour,
  Lend me your tongues to speak,
Some word of love, some word of praise,
  For mine are all too weak.

My God, my Father, Friend, my All,
  How sweet this hour to me,
What feast of love of heav'nly light,
  These moments spent with Thee,
Ah, words my Jesus cannot tell,
  The rapture of this union,
Whilst Thou art mine and I all Thine
  In this one sweet communion.

Sweet echoes, return ! thou'rt mine, all mine !
　In wonderful whispers sweet !
Yea, Lord, in my heart I'll ne'er repine,
　While faithful my watch I keep !

Yes, he that hath ears to hear, can hear
　Those whispers of sweetest love.
They soothe every sad and weary tear,
　They tell us of joys above.

They come to the rich and to the poor,—
　The palace and cot the same;
The breath of God it shall still endure
　To soothe e'en the blind and lame.

It sometimes falleth in accents mild,
　In sorrow and tears and song;
Oh, Lord, make our faith like to a child,
　The praise unto Thee belong !

And when the last whisper comes to all,
　Oft sooner than heart e'er dreamed,
Oh, may we all welcome His loving call,
　"Come to Me, thou art redeemed !"

OH, ICY HEART OF WINTER!

OH, icy heart of Winter drear,
    I've known thy blighting breath !
For then my boy was called from here
    To mystic realms of Death.

Oh, dids't thou deem him all too grand,
    Too pure for taint of sin !
Then called him to you Summer Land
    Where all may enter in.

Ah ! though in Winter was his flight,
    And Winter rules us now,
Still he was Thine by every right,—
    Unto Thy will we bow.

His dear eyes had that far-off look ;
    I called him angel child !
A voice, as of a singing brook,
    Was his, and mien so mild.

Oh, God of that bright Summer Land
    Whose flowers forever bloom,
We know he's numbered with that band
    That fear not Winter's gloom !

And though in Winter we should go
  To meet our own above,
Thy smile will keep us all aglow
  With purity and love.

TO A FIRE-FLY.

GUARDIAN of the Summer night,
    With your lantern's winking light,
Searching under dusky leaves,
Tangled vines, and cottage eaves,
When the cricket's shrilly cheep
Warns you that the world's asleep !
Here, at daylight, dull and slow,
Not one gleam of gold you show.

In your bronze-brown garb again,
Straggling o'er a leaf's green plain,
Who could guess, by any art,
The warm glow that fills your heart ?
So a friend may wander by
While our sunshine still is high ;
But, when shadows fall around,
Steadfast, warm and true be found.

So the love that hidden lies
Wakes to glad our•heart and eyes,
When adversity draws near,
And false love-lights disappear.
Cheering all the starlit calm ;
Rover 'mid the musky balm ;
Restless, pulsing, sudden spark ;
Summer's jewel in the dark.

AUTUMN RAIN.

A WEIRD, monotonous refrain,
    O'er sodden leaves, black with their blight,
As the fingers of the Northwind smite
    The tense, steel harp-strings of the rain !

AT TWILIGHT.

WHEN, at twilight, oft I ponder
  On the Future and the Past,
Thinking deeply, then I wonder
  Will these shadows always last?

Are there no bright days before me?
  In the darkness must I wait?
Will the clouds be always o'er me?
  Mine a sad and cruel fate?

Star-like Hope afar is beaming,
  Whispering : " All will be well ! "
But perhaps my heart is dreaming,
  Ever dreaming,—who can tell?

Patiently I muse, nor murmur ;
  Life is but a brittle thread ;
Yet my strength would be the firmer
  If bright pathways I could tread.

Why, oh, why this heart's wild beating?
  Why this tumult in my breast?
Father, unto Thee retreating,
  I would crave thy Peace and Rest.

THE ÆSTHETIC CROWS.

"CAW! Caw!" beside a fallow field
    A band of old crows sat ;
The good old farmer planted corn.
    They looked askance at that ;
"Caw! Caw!" when he departs, cried they
    "We'll find out what he's at."

The noonday sun grew high and hot.
    The farmer quit his task ;
And then the crows,—to speak it so,—
    Threw off their simple mask,
And carried off that farmer's corn ;
    His leave they didn't ask.

Now, what they couldn't eat that day,
    They buried for the next ;
So, when that good old farmer came,
    He stood awhile perplexed ;
And, though a man of manners mild,
    Was evidently vexed.

Thought he, " a scare-crow I'll set up
    Their knavish tricks to stop ;
I'll rig me up one instantly,
    Before more corn I drop ;
Until I drive these thieves away
    How can I raise a crop? "

He stuffed a worn out suit with straw,
  And propped it up straightway ;
The crows that dotted all the woods
  Looked down in grim dismay.
"Ha ! Ha !" the farmer chuckled then,
  "I don't think, now, they'll stay !"

But when the farmer left his field
  They brought his stolen corn,
And laid it in the holes again,
  With actions quite forlorn ;
"What have we done," cried they, "to meet
  With such bucolic scorn ?

"Our punishment is much to sad ;
  We are not driven hence ;
And for this farmer's well-meant jest,
  We make this recompense ;
That we'd mistake this for a man,
  Shocks our artistic sense."

That farmer's corn grew tall and thick,
  And waved in tasseled pride ;
But never since that day have crows
  His field with envy eyed.
He couldn't guess the reason why,
  I don't believe he tried.

IN MEMORIAM.

(LAURA DE GRAFF.)

BUD of promise, our heart's treasure,
    Chilled by blighting frosts of earth !
Faded hopes,—Ah, who can measure,
    Who describe the lonely hearth ?

Yet, 'tis by these sacred flowers,—
    These angelic lives sublime,
Showing here God-given powers,
    That we prove a Life divine.

We shall meet, to part, ah, never !
    When we walk those streets of gold,
Where those buds shall bloom forever
    In the loving Saviour's fold.

Darling, though our hearts are broken,
    Though our Laura's voice is still,
We'll remember Christ hath spoken,
    He will yet His words fulfill !

LOVE.

WHENCE is the mystical power thou dost
wield,
From sin and sorrow my being to shield?
Hovering o'er me, like Angelic wing,
Soothing the cares that each morrow may bring.
Earth seems a bower, all beauteous and bright,
When Love sheds o'er us its pure, happy light.

Love lifts our burdens and dries all our tears,
Chases away all our sorrows and fears ;
Sweetly and merrily Time glides along,
Filling our days with enchantment and song.
Clouds of the tempest can ne'er hover near,
When the dear voice of our loved one we hear.

Stay then, oh, Love ! with thy rapturous gleams,
Shed o'er Life's journey thy blest, starry beams !
Ecstasy filleth my soul, as I list
Unto thy voice, in the deepening mist !
While thy blest halo of infinite light
Quickens my soul with its wakening might.

Love ! while thine accents so tenderly fall,
Thrilling my heart with their mystical call,

Gladly thy summons I haste to obey,—
Love ! in thy presence each moment I'd stay !
Sweet is the voyage, down Life's rippling tide,
When thou, oh, dearest, art here by my side !

Time cannot bring me one wearisome day,—
Love-light can charm every shadow away.
In thy dear face I read all that is best,
In thine arms' shelter, I find peace and rest.
Kindred or friendship can never compare,
Love ! with the rapture beside thee I share !

Oh, the wild thrill in the clasp of thy hand,
Quickens the ardor that Friendship had fanned !
Now, as I gaze in thy dear, tender eyes,
Clearly I see the fond love that ne'er dies.
Truer and nobler than station or fame,—
Brighter and richer, is Love's gentle flame !

Then sweetly caress me, my darling, my own,
Whatever betide, I am thine, thine alone !
Oh, what is our life but the darkest unrest
Love ! without thee and thy sympathy blest !
Welcome is Death, and its dark, dark eclipse,
Love ! with thy kisses of joy on our lips !

When, at last, to our gaze the sad angel appears,
And slowly our barque yonder silent shore nears,
Where loved ones are standing to welcome us o'er,
Where trouble and sorrow shall blight us no more,
The Father we'll know, in blest mansions above,
Whose Name is forever the symbol of *Love.*

"MEMORIAL DAY."

I.

OVER valley and plain where our heroes re-
pose,
We have strewn the bright garlands of spring,
And the pure, dewy tears of the lily and rose
On their graves with sweet sympathy cling !

II.

In each veteran's heart what proud memories wake,
As the loud, steady tramp dies away.
When he thinks of the comrades for whose hallowed
sake,
He has kept this Memorial Day.

III.

They are camped where the sunlight of glory is
shed,
And the storm-cloud of battle no more
Shall thunder its fury their ranks overhead;
The march with its tumult is o'er.

IV.

But how proud is the heritage left to our land,
Oh, the deeds that they wrought are enscrolled
On the still growing stars of our banner so grand,
And their blood has made pure every fold.

V.

They are living, though dead, in the nation we
      love,
   In the hearts of a people they breathe,
And the stars of our standard gleams down from
      above
   O'er the shrines that our garlands enwreathe.

VI.

So proudly we speak of the heroes that fell
   In the years that have rolled far away,
And forever the nation their story shall tell
   On its deathless Memorial Day !

"FOLLOW ME !"

I WOULD that the Saviour might come to our
      home,
   As He came, in those days of yore.
We know that His spirit from Heaven doth roam,
   And waits for us long at the door.

He sayeth, as then, " Follow me !   Follow me !
   Confide all your sorrows and care !"
Yea, Lord, all the day we have trusted in Thee,
   Thou'lt help us Life's burdens to bear.

Oh, carry His word to the office, the store,
  The factory, the school which we seek !
To the farm or the city, or 'mid ocean's roar,
  He's with us each day of the week.

For "Lo ! am I not with you always," He said,
  "Even unto the end of the world !
I was crucified, buried, and rose from the dead,
  That the sin from thy heart might be hurled !"

All round us we witness His presence and power,
  In earth and in sky and in air;
All nature inspires us, and to Thee this hour
  Our thoughts are ascending in prayer.

He came unto Mary and Martha, so pure,
  He sympathized, too, with their care,
He came upon earth mortal ills to endure,
  And all weary burdens to bear.

He knows our affairs, all our troubles and needs,
  His judgment excels all else here;
He who paints the sunsets, our inmost thought
    reads,
  He loveth His children, so dear.

In Him who adorneth the wing of the bird,
  Forever on earth we can trust;
Oh, joyful the hour when His name first we heard,
  We feel that His wisdom is just.

We know, if we faithfully walk by His side,
   And link our thoughts unto His life,
All contamination will ever subside,
   And calm will replace every strife.

And, when the last journey shall unto us come,
   We'll hear that celestial strain,—
"Follow me, I will guide you to yon Heavenly
     Home,
   Your heritage, faithful, to gain."

Through clouds, and through space, we will " Fol-
     low Thee," Lord !
   Thou glorious Leader, so grand !
Great Pathfinder, may we take Thee at Thy word
   And go at Thy loving command !

SPIRIT VOICES.

HARK ! the hallowed spirit voices !
   Hear that glad and Heavenly strain,
Coming, in sweet, whispered echoes
   To our weary hearts again.
Bless the dear ones there united,
   Joining in seraphic praise,
Where the white robed Angels ever
   Unto Him their voices raise !

CHORUS.

Oh, the music softly falling,
   Like the stir of Angel wings !
Hark the spirit voices calling
   From Thy realm, oh, King of Kings !

They are calling, sweetly calling,
   Unto those they love the best,
Bidding them to banish sorrow,
   Telling them of promised rest.
Be not deaf unto that music ;
   Open wide the spirit's door ;
Soon our spirits, too, will join them,
   Praising God forevermore.

Sing aloud, ye seraph songsters !
   Sing from yonder sainted Land !
Songs from you have thrilled our heart-strings ;
   We shall soon among you stand.
Watch, ye guardian Angels, o'er us ;
   Shield us with your holy love ;
Spirit voices, o'er us hover,
   Lead us to yon realms above !

THE ONE THAT I ADORE.

DEEP in my heart there is a face
   So bright, so sweet, so fair !
Adorned with every lovely grace,—
   Through Life I'll keep it there.
She brings to me the fondest dreams
   That all my joys restore ;
My star, my rose, till Life shall close,—
   The one that I adore.

CHORUS.

Faithful and true, bright as the dew,
   That gems the lilies o'er ;
Ever my own,—mine, mine, mine alone,—
   The one that I adore.

My truest love to her I give ;
   My Life she soon will bless ;
In sunlight of her smiles I live,
   For me is each caress.
The birds that sing in Summer skies
   Her praises warble o'er ;
Oh, dear to me, while Life shall be,—
   The one that I adore !

No other lips could ever woo
   My dear one from my side !
Oh she has promised to be true
   Through all this world so wide !
Were she an Angel from above,
   I could not love her more,—
My soul's delight, so peerless, bright,—
   The one that I adore !

BEREAVEMENT.

THE Hand that smites,—to it I bow ;
   Yet awful its decree !
E'en while my heart is bleeding now,
   God's wisdom I can see ;
And, though the blow is hard to bear,
   And dreary is Life's way,
I still must own His loving care
   That folds me, day by day.

Sad heart, He knew how weak we were,
   How faithless, and how blind.
Though bitter tears mine eyes oft blur,
   Still, Father, thou art kind.
Thou saw'st rough ways before my child,
   Where these weak arms would fail.
Thou, ere his mind could be defiled,
   Did'st lift him from earth's vale.

He dwells with Angels bright and fair
    Where grief nor shadows come ;
Eternal glories he doth share
    In Thy celestial Home.
There, lovingly he waits for me !
    I see, in every star,
Those eyes that look so patiently
    To welcome me afar.

Oh, precious joy, beyond all bliss
    To motherhood e'er given,
The one sweet thought I bear,—'tis this,—
    I have a child in Heaven.
Yea, though from me thou'rt far away,
    In yonder realms of joy,
I know with God I'll find, some day,
    My darling angel boy !

MARCH.

OH ! a wild " harum-scarum " is March;
    He tweaks every nose he meets,
In a way that he thinks quite arch,
    While he whistles o'er woods and streets.
Then he shouts down the chimneys high,
    With a gleeful and grim " Ho ! Ho ! "
And sifts, from the blustry sky,
    Such a flurry of blinding snow !

" Now I'll rage like a lion ! " roars he,
    And he rattles the icy trees:
" Then as mild as a lamb I'll be,
    These valleys and hills to please.
Soon I'll waken the snow-drops fair,
    Just to hint of the sweet days near;
Then the pretties away I'll scare,
    With a frown, and a shriek so drear ! "

Oh ! a " happy-go-lucky " is March,
    But we laugh at his hearty glee,
For we know that his tricks, so arch,
    Are the promise of joys to be.
Let him scatter his flossy snow;
    Let him rattle the branches high;
Ah ! his sister, sweet April, we know,
    Soon will peep out of yon blue sky !

A HEN'S COLUMBIAN LAY.

"CLUCK ! Cluck ! my darlings pretty,
    If fowls are wise or witty,
The race that we belong to doesn't show it, dears;
    Your mother wants to teach you,
    In tones she hopes will reach you,
A most important fact, and you shall know it, dears.

    Why bipeds of no feather
    Should jubilate together,
And leave the chickens out, to me a mystery is;
    Though fowls of low condition,
    I hold that our position
Ranks high with those who know what Spanish
        history is.

    I don't say, chicks, we aided
    In anything which they did
Who sent Columbus o'er the seas meandering;
    But what at first suggested
    A new world's not contested ;
Why are we overlooked in this philandering ?

    We *don't* plume ourselves much on
    Our family escutcheon;
But, speaking of Columbus, incidentally,

Your ancestor it was
That helped along his cause,
She laid the egg he used experimentally !

REMEMBERED.

LIKE a bird, when pursued by the hunter's keen
arrow
It timidly flies to its home in the nest,
So my heart, even now, from the world cold and
narrow,
Will fondly seek thine for its haven of rest.

For I know that the innocent love which I cherish
Is something diviner than earth can bestow;
And alloy can not reach it, the gem can not perish,
My heart still shall wear it wherever I go.

'Tis the unsevered link that Heaven doth bind us,
'Tis richer than riches that dower the sea;
The sweet bliss of Paradise surely will find us,
And that will atone for all sorrows to me.

There, an infinite God will bring true hearts to-
gether,
And fondly we'll roam in His gardens above.
And no envy can make of Life there a blank
heather,
For His name is the symbol of infinite Love !

SUGGESTED BY THE PLAY OF
"INGOMAR."

HOW many hearts are sold and bought,
   Or by sacrifices won ?
How few " with but one single thought,—
   Two hearts that beat as one !"

Methinks, when two hearts thus are blest,
   They're stamped with Heaven's seal !
Thus they enjoy, in Life, sweet rest;
   Their lives are true and leal.

And, when the silver threads appear,
   They still go hand in hand;
Old age still makes their hearts more dear,—
   They've honored God's command.

Oh, Ingomar, 'twas your blest fate
   To win as few have done.
To symbol,—sweetheart, wife and mate,—
   " Two hearts that beat as one !"

And when your Master from on high
   Calls,—Life's race grandly won,—
Oh, answer : 'Tis not Death to die !
   " Hearts still shall beat as one !"

THE SILENT BOATMAN.

OH, Boatman, come hither from yonder bright
        shore,
  And guide my frail barque o'er the way !
I longingly wait for the raptures in store,
  Come over, and hasten, I pray.
For the keel of thy boat, as it leaveth the strand,
  And the dip of the oars now I list,
How long will it be ere it toucheth the land,
  Seen bright through the deepening mist ?

When once I have crossed o'er the dark, chilly tide,
  'Mid shadows, so gloomy and deep,
When safely I'm anchored on yon radiant side,
  I know that no more I shall weep.
Oh, long I've been waiting for that golden key
  To open the white, pearly gate !
I know that my darling ones there I shall see,
  I feel for my coming they wait !

Oh, soon be unbarred those grand portals of day,
  That Jesus' dear face I may see !
When sentinel Angels, in brightest array,
  Will quickly give welcome to me.

How gladly I'll join that celestial host,
    Their jubilant music to sing;
In praise to the Father, the Son, Holy Ghost,
    My glad hallelujahs will ring !

Oh, darling one, resting in Jesus' dear arms,
    And folded on His gentle breast,
To you I shall go, from the world's weary storms,
    And my spirit with you shall find rest !
A bond of reunion, a more perfect love,
    Will follow the wearisome *Now;*
I feel that when fondly you meet me above
    With garlands you'll wreathe my pale brow.

No eye hath e'er seen, and no lips now can tell
    Of joys that our God hath prepared.
Oh, world weary spirit, He doeth all well,—
    The Saviour your sorrow hath shared !
And now, as the Boatman is sailing to me,
    I know I shall safely cross o'er,
For His hand guides the rudder, I plainly can see,
    To rest and to gladness once more !

DAWN.

(SONNET.)

GRASSES o'erbent with globes of tremulous
        dew
  That slip to earth, when tricksy winds go by,
  And leave the lithe, unglossy green still dry.
Pure, honeyed breath of flowers, fresh and new,
And melting clouds disclosing burnished blue,
    As if the deep, illimitable sky
    Were new-born! Hark! from petaled shelter
      nigh,
To seek lost sunset's interrupted clew,
Comes crooning now the bee, with sinuous sweep,
    Like silver, smiting silver, bird-songs ring,
      And plashing rills, with turbulence headlong,
Gush from the hillside's mossed and lichened steep.
    "A new day!" birds and bees and breezes sing;
      A new day, oh, my heart, for Hope, Love,
      Joy and Song!

SNOW.

A NET–WORK of dark boughs
    Along the dull gray sky;
A flinty road whereon the wheels are creaking as
      they go;
    A scuffle and a shout
    Of winds that hurry by,
A fen, with frozen hoof-dints, and a brook with
      silent flow.

    A broken, roadside wall,
    With draggling, rusty vines;
A tawny hay-mow crouching, like a lion, by the
      hill;
    Weird tracery of ice
    Among a group of pines,
And, in the vale, a farm-house, strange, desolate
      and still.

A landscape overhung with ever-changing flakes
    That whirl in slumberous eddies, and loiteringly
      fall;
A drift that sweeps along, till in powdery mist it
      breaks;
    Now gradually vanish, the road, the fields, and
      all.

Oh, sunlight of the heart, amid this wintry blight !
How, at my will, the pleasant Summer sounds
and pictures throng;
The homeward-wending cows—a face in waning
light,—
A world of waving greenery,—the bluebird's
fluted song !

DON'T YOU HEAR THE ROBIN?

DON'T you hear the robin,
Singing down the dell?
Oh, the loving message
Now he comes to tell !
Gone is all the sighing,
Past the weary hours ;
Hey, for buds and blossoms,
Glad and jeweled showers.
Greenly waves the willow,
Mirth is on the air ;
Oh, the happy music
For each heart to share.
While the silver brooklets
Run, the joy to tell,—
Don't you hear the robin
Singing down the dell?
Happy, happy robin,
Singing down the dell !

Don't you hear the robin,
   Singing, heart of mine?
Joy and Hope are beaming,
   Why should we repine?
Hark ! the bird that brings you
   Brighter days to live !—
Tells you of the sunshine
   That will blessings give !
See the rosy blossoms
   Showered from the tree ;
Over emerald meadows
   Hear the sounds of glee.
" Joy !" the sky is breathing,
   " Joy " the rivers tell ;
Don't you hear the robin
   Singing down the dell?
Happy, happy robin,
   Singing down the dell !

GRANDMA'S GLASSES.

SHE tells me just the strangest things
　　About the times of long ago, —
And oft of them a song she sings ;
　　'Tis wonderful what grandmas' know.

She talks of cities she has seen,
　　And of their people quaint and queer ;
I wonder where she hasn't been ;
　　Her stories, too, I love to hear.

Something that's new, each day I'm told,
　　I love on grandma's face to look, —
It never, to my mind, grows old,
　　It seems to me a picture book.

I linger long beside her chair,
　　And, tho' a child of just twice three,
If I could grandma's glasses wear,
　　Maybe I'd see what she can see !

THEY ARE NOT DEAD.

THEY are not dead, but slumber, now,
   No anguish can they feel ;
Bright Glory's crown is on each brow,
   Where Death hath set its seal.
No breath of sorrow clouds their way,
   No discord can they hear ;
In portals bright of endless day
   God's anthems greet the ear.

Since Jesus died and rose for them,
   What fear they, past the grave?
Faith is their radiant diadem,—
   He perished us to save.
To join the bright and ransomed throng
   Their loved ones long have led,
Glad welcomed by the Angels' song,
   They sleep !—they are not dead !

With Hope and Love and Purity
   They lived their homes to bless ;
And in God's dear security
   Found peace and happiness.
What though our hearts are aching now
   Sore with their stricken woe?
All to the Hand that smites must bow,—
   The gain is theirs, we know.

Oh, let them silent, peaceful sleep,
   They're safely Home, at last !
Why should we mourn,—why should we weep?
   Earth-anguish they have passed !
They watch us, through the windowed stars ;
   Their mem'ry blesses here.
No storm their tranquil being mars,—
   The loved, the good, the dear !

Father of earth, of Heaven above,
   Though strong this mortal bond,
May all clasp hands, in holy love,
   The spirit land beyond.
Rest to each form that lowly lies,
   Their grass we softly tread ;
What though the floral tribute dies,—
   They sleep !—they are not Dead !

A WORLD'S-FAIR MEMORY.

OH, friend, do you remember yet,
    When 'neath the lofty dome we met,
In that White City far away
That thronged with people grave and gay?

I know you think of one sweet face
That wore a mother's lovelit grace.
I know her words, again you hear,—
Those words of trust and faith, so dear.
'Twas where uprose, majestic, grand,
The sculptured forms, on either hand,
Of *Christ* the Saviour of the earth,
And *Lincoln*, Freedom's soul of worth!

We gazed on Him, the blest, the meek,
With awe-struck hearts that scarce could speak,
As dumb as sculptured marble we
In presence of such majesty,
Wrought by the hand of Genius there
With Art that was beyond compare!
What thoughts we had of Christ, the Lord,
I felt we held in sweet accord.
What thoughts of him who freed the slave,—
God's champion, the true, the brave,—

Whose words were " Charity towards all ! "
Ah ! friend of mine, do you recall ?

Then spake dear mother-lips, " I'll wait
Your coming, be it soon or late,
The Saviour of his land between
And the world-saving *Nazarene.*
Not safer could a mother be
'Twixt Time and vast Eternity ! "

And there we found that gentle heart,
Wrapped in her thoughts, from all apart.
A halo seemed to crown her face
With all its motherhood and grace.
Her woman nature, upright, just,
Had spoken words of perfect trust ;
And, as we gazed, she seemed to be
Akin to sculptured majesty,
And imaged him who freed the slave,
And *Christ* who came the world to save !

THE TOUCH OF GOD.

'TIS the finger of God that hath touched me,
    It bids me awake and arise,
To look not for happiness earthward,
    But yonder in Heavenly skies.

'Tis His hand which hath tenderly smitten,
    Through gloom of the gathering night ;
His voice 'tis that calleth " Come upward,
    For I am the Way and the Light ! "

Shall I not give my trust in His keeping ;
    Though narrow and dark is the way,
I feel that His blest hand is guiding
    My footsteps to yon perfect day.

My faith liveth past all affliction.
    I bow to His chastening rod.
Oh, may I behold, in Life's sorrows,
    The touch of the finger of God !

LOVE'S DREAM OF THE FUTURE.

OH, sweet, new Love that comes to bloom
    Within a Life of hopeless gloom !
Oh, sweet, dear Love that comes to bless
A Life that had been purposeless !
What rapture, as of Spring's pure thrill
Rejuvinating vale and hill !
What glory, as of sunset skies
With tints of God's own Paradise,
Illuming the twilight hour
With Peace and Hope and wondrous power !
A new Life in the Future shone
For two brave hearts to live, alone !
Two hearts, entwined, to do and dare,
All struggles, earthly hopes, to share,
Till God shall join their pathways here,
With bonds that link, as sphere to sphere,
The stars that gem the vast above
In Love, immutable sweet Love!
Not only for this Life of earth,
Not only for its dross and dearth,
Not only linked for this, ah, no !
But still beneath God's smile to be
One through His grand Eternity !

Oh, flowers of earth, ye fade and die !
Fast fades the bloom of Summer's sky,
Its sweetest roses withered lie
   Ere snows of Winter fall !
But Love's unfading, fragrant bloom
Endures when skies are hid in gloom,
And blossoms far beyond the tomb ;
   Love dieth not at all !

For 'tis of God, the gift is given,
For 'tis an attribute of Heaven !
Though earth and all therein be riven,
   And fade yon stars above,
True Love shall ever be the same,
Dear Love its own shall fondly claim
And still return from whence it came,—
   To God, for God is Love !

Two hearts that met, upon Life's way,
When all their songs were sweet and gay ;
Yet disappointment, bitter, dark,
Had made their deathless love an ark !—
A shelter from the storms of Life,
Its unremitting pains and strife.
Both equal in His gifts divine,
Health, strength, and talents to outshine
The common throng that plod each day ;
Both firm resolved to conquer wrong
And sing, at last, the victor's song !

Within each other's eyes they read
God's message, and it softly said :
" One purpose shall be ours, one thought,
One human destiny be wrought ;
However Fate may intervene
We know the hand of the Unseen
Will join their lives, in His own time,
If not on earth, in realms sublime."

Oh, dream of yonder Future sweet
That would make both their lives complete !
They lived but in each other's smile,
Two souls without a thought of guile ;
The agony, as of the cross,
To each, would be the other's loss !

Though sorrow fell,—their hopes were dust—
This still perfected their dear trust
In one another !
            From God's home
His loving angels seemed to roam,
And bear from each to each a word,—
A chord of sympathy to quell
The shadows that around them fell,
And draw them nearer, could this be,
Through deepest, purest sympathy !
For God had smiled upon their love,
And all His angels far above !
They knew it by that hallowed sign
Which only souls of Love divine !

That love which pulsates through each breast,
In gladness or in grief's unrest,
In unison, sublime, supreme,
Till lived for them the Future's dream !
All thought of self had left each heart,
One thought,—Love, " Love, where'er *thou* art."

Oh, spirits, that nor time, nor space
Can through Eternity displace !
The Future shall unite them there
In bliss, in rapture past compare.
What is the separation sad
To this reunion, endless, glad ?
One, living in each other's eyes,
Through gardens of His Paradise !
One, smiled upon by Deity
For Love that still could faithful be
Through Time, and all its burdens deep,—
Its heartfelt pangs, and eyes that weep,—
Its longing, yearning, anguished thrall !
One soul, one heart, past all recall,
After earth's travail, crowneth all !

  Oh, Love, they may not tell the bliss,—
    The rapture of the heart,
  When on their lips they feel thy kiss
    Its holy seal impart !
  To know that one dear soul is true,
    Through all of weal or woe,
  Each heart girds up its strength anew
    To plod Life's path below.

A life ideal meets their gaze,—
    A life through years to be,—
Along the sweet sequestered ways
    Of Love's unfathomed sea !
To read in eyes that watched so long
    The bliss of meeting's thrill,
Would turn all sadness into song
    Life's waste with roses fill !

A Life's ideal, this shall guide
    Their steps while on they go,
Till they shall wander, side by side,
    In youth's unfading glow ;
Clasped in God's boundless, infinite
    Beatitude above.
Forever blest, for aye at rest
    With Him whose name is Love !

IN MEMORY.

HENRY P. UNDERHILL. DIED IN BALTIMORE,
OCTOBER 4TH, 1889.

(TO HIS COMRADES OF THE G. A. R.)

OH, hearts that saw that manly heart
Consigned to mother earth !
'Tis meet to give a word of praise
To bravery and worth.
Love was the countersign he bore
To yonder realms afar ;
His memory is ours to-day,
As bright as evening's star.

Recall we now the battlefield,
Where, 'mid the storied brave,
He stood the storm of shot and shell
The dear old flag to save.
Oh, comrades of the G. A. R.,
His deeds you treasure now,
While o'er the sod that hides his form
You pause with sorrowing brow !

Though but a child in those dark days,
I hear again the tread
Of soldiers brave, as slow they come
Bearing a Nation's dead.

And he was there to tribute pay
   Unto a comrade dear ;
That song : "He's crossed the river dark,"
   Falls softly on mine ear.

The grand old anthem then was heard,
   In accents loud and clear,
When lips of his so bravely spoke :
   "Let's from the children hear !"
In civic ranks renowned and high,
   He lives, though cold he lies.
Oh, brothers of the Mason's craft,
   His love bedims your eyes !

A soul of worth gone up to God,
   A bright exemplar left !
While thoughts of him live in our hearts
   We cannot be bereft.
Bearing his honors, bravely won,
   He sleeps beneath the trees ;
The flag he loved his winding sheet,
   His psalm the whispering breeze .

Upon that soldiers' monument
   His hands have helped to rear,
Inscribe his name in memory,
   And drop a soldier's tear.
Beside his loved ones, he's at rest,
   And this slight tribute take
From one who while a tiny child
   Loved him for Country's sake.

PRAYER.

WHEN the twilight shadows gather,
   And a mantle o'er us flings,
In a prayer what soothing comfort,
   Oh, what peace and rest it brings !
What is more divine and holy
   Than a voice that whispers there :
"Cast your burdens on Me ever,
   I am willing all to bear !"

Blessed words, Thou crowned with glory,—
   Once despiséd Nazarene !
Crucified to bring all sinners
   To that Home no eye hath seen.
Let us cast our troubles on Him,—
   All our doubts and unbelief,
Let us worship and adore Him,—
   He will take away our grief.

He will calm Life's fiercest battle,
   End the tumult and the strife ;
He became our burden-bearer,
   Laying down His precious life !
Then unto Him songs and praises
   Let the heart bring everywhere !
And adore Him for His mercies
   While we kneel to Him in prayer.

Father, kindly look upon us,
   Shield us with Thy love divine !
May we, through Life's weary journey,
   In our hearts Thy name enshrine.
And, when days of earth are ended,—
   When we reach thy mansion fair,—
We shall know the hallowed blessings
   We have gained by earnest prayer.

SABBATH EVE.

OH, Sabbath eve, blest Sabbath eve,
   When all the cares of Life we leave !
When in sweet quiet hearts repose
Far from the week's unrest and woes.
'Tis then we nearer seem to be
To Him who reigns eternally.
A glory lovely and divine
Makes earth a pure and holy shrine !
Awake, ye hallowed tones, once more,—
Ring out, ye bells, from shore to shore !
Wake sons of men, and anthems raise,
To God on high be endless praise.
From deep to deep resound the song,
And Heavenly choirs the strain prolong.
Thy calm may every heart receive,
Oh, Sabbath eve, blest Sabbath eve !

Oh, Sabbath eve, dear Sabbath eve,
To all on earth a sweet reprieve !
When hearts with toil and sorrow bow,
A messenger of Peace art thou.
Now weary hands from Labor rest,
And joy returns,—a welcome guest.
A holiness, on earth, in air,
Falls round us, like the breath of prayer ;
And every heart is called above
To God, the fount of Light and Love !
Oh, golden clasp to bind the week,—
May every heart thy glory speak ;
Let grateful prayers, like incense, rise
To Him who rules the earth and skies.
Dear boon of joy to souls that grieve,—
Oh, Sabbath eve, blest Sabbath eve !

BE PURE IN SPEECH.

How vast is the sphere of humanity's voice,
  Approaching the Power Divine !
Communing with God, and with Angels, and man,
  How mighty its sense to define.
The first spoken words that were heard o'er the
    earth
  Were God's command : " Let there be light ! "
When, from the beginning, from chaos he made
  The beautiful Day and the Night.

Ah ! " Music hath charms," likewise Painting,—
    in Art
  What wonderful things we behold !
But all of their beauties must ever be crowned
  With words, that are grander than gold.
Alas ! for the voice that with anger is heard,—
The harshest of accents it hath ;
Oh, cultivate silvery sounds in our speech,—
  " The soft answer turneth 'way wrath ! "

Oh, wondrous the power that lies in the tongue !
  In sickness, and sorrow and gloom,
It falls, like the touch of an Angelic hand,
  To lighten the loneliest room !

And sweet are kind words to the laboring ones
    Which give them the praise they have won ;
Remember the words of the Master who said :
    "Oh, good, faithful servant, well done !"

While guiding the young with the truest of words,
    Fulfilling our mission of love,—
Dissuading from evil, with tenderest tones,—
    We're leading their footsteps above.
And, when about others around us we speak,
    Let's never say aught that is ill ;
For scandal is ever the discord of Life,
    Its bane and its enemy still.

The suppliant voice that would reach to the
    Throne,—
    With power approach the divine,—
Should never descend unto accents obscene,
    But Good should its music refine.
Oh, pure be our speech, that when days have
    waxed old,
    And locks are as white as the snow,
When wrinkled the brow, and with tottering steps
    All feeble and trembling we go,

May we then be known by a sweet, kindly voice,
    That falls like the mild, vesper bell ;
And tho' it in Death shall grow evermore still
    Its echo soft music shall tell.

Anew let us culture these Heavenly sounds
 The purest of thoughts to express ;
Let gentleness, truth and the kindliest love
 Guard words that shall fall but to bless !

SHADOWS.

I.

WHY do these shadows encircle my way?
 Why do they denser grow, day after day?
Why must my heart that was once gay and light,
Now be enshrouded in the gloom of the night?

God of the helpless, oh, send me one ray !
Let not my life be as one cast away.
Grant Thou a few years of Peace, Hope and Rest !
Thy will, not mine, Lord, for Thou knowest best !

II.

Out of the darkness and into the Light,
Lead us, oh, Saviour, by day and by night !
Out of the tempest of Death and of blight,
Guide us from Time to Eternity's height.

Thou art the Light, thro' this valley of pain,
Star of our Hope, never gleaming in vain.
Hush thy repining, oh, sad heart of mine,
Gaze on the Light that is fadeless, Divine !

SUNSET.

THE sun is slowly sinking, now, behind the
crimson clouds,
The night is coming down the sky, with mantle
that enshrouds;
And as the twilight shadows o'er my spirit softly
steal,
I'm thinking of my darling one, and sad of heart I
feel.

Oh, shall I see him soon again, amid that Angel
choir?
I yearn to clasp him with a mother's infinite desire!
Oh, can he see my anguish,—read my lonely, aching heart?
Oh, doth he realize my loss since doomed from him
to part?

Oh, Georgie, how we miss thee, dear divinely gifted
boy!
We wonder how we live without thee, for thou
wast our joy!
If God had not defended with His everlasting
power,
Methinks a sadly burdened mind would be thy
mother's dower.

But matchless is His mercy, and His pure and
    deathless love,
And thro' and thro' my being hath He words of
    comfort wove !
Yea, in this spirit I arouse, and courage now I take,
And bear the cross that He hath given, for my
    darling's sake.

No matter what this life may give, nor aught that
    blesses here,
No happiness can come to me, and earth can never
    cheer,
For thou art gone, my sweeter self, my dearest
    one, my all !
Oh, sad indeed the mother-heart that sorrows dark
    enthrall !

The Future loometh ever lone, without thee by my
    side.
I never dreamed but through the years thou
    wouldst with me abide.
I cannot fathom now my loss : Oh, shall I never
    see
Thy darling, angel face again ?   Alas ! and can this
    be ?

      Protect me now, thou Angel fair,
        And watch above me here ;
      For while thy precious love I share,
        Yon Heaven seems more near !

I pray that God may send me peace,
    And strength to banish fear,—
Until my soul shall find release,
    And we meet, Georgie dear !

Oh, meet me, darling, at the gate,
    And take me by the hand ;
Tell Jesus, not to say " Too late !"
    To join thee in that Land.

And now Good-night ! thou Angel bird !
    Night holds the starry dome ;
When I awake, may new strength gird
    My soul to reach thy Home.

WHY DO I LOVE?

WHY do I love my love so well?
    Why doth thy image ever dwell
Within my soul, all fears to quell
All doubts to hide, ah, who can tell?
Why do I love my love so well?
In accents sweet thy voice I hear,
Though far away, yet thou art near;
In whispering heartfelt notes, so clear,
Our vows we plight from year to year,
Why do I hold my love so dear?

CHORUS.

Why do I love?   Why do I love?
   Why do I love thee dear so well?
Summers may come, summers depart,
   Every sweet flower could the secret tell,
Why does each star shine from afar
   Why does the rill sing down the dell?
Faithful is he, loving but me,
   That's why I love my love so well!

Ask why the rosebuds love the dew;
Or why the sunset's glorious hue
Bespangles Heaven's own spotless blue!
Or why the stars their light renew!
That's why I love my love so true!
Question the birds of air that sing
Why do they greet the jeweled spring;
Or bid the blossoms while they cling.
Tell why such joy to earth they bring,
I'll answer then, my own, my king.

DISAPPOINTMENT.

BEND, proud spirit, 'neath the burden;
  Life must disappointments bear !
Murmur not when they have fallen,
  Naught can stay the hand of care.
Yield with trustfulness and meekness,
  Clouds will come to brightest skies !
And a chastening sorrow may be
  But a blessing in disguise.

God, the Monitor of Heaven
  Holds the scepter in His hand !
Though the earth may crush thy spirit,
  He, to save, is true and grand !
Up, and meekly bear Life's burdens;
  Be not in thy anguish bowed !
Look beyond, and see the glorious
  Silver lining to each cloud.

PASSION VERSUS LOVE.

THE Heart has its turbulent passion,
    The heart has its beautiful Love;
While one is the world's daily fashion,
    The other descends from Above !

Oh, passion is brief and is fleeting,
    But Love it endureth through Life !
The soul it awakes at its greeting,
    It banishes sorrow and strife.

What bliss, through the long, weary hours
    To know that one heart is your own,
Oh, Life is a garden of flowers
    That, loveless, was weary and lone !

Should passion e'er come to allure you,
    Oh, bid it begone while you may !
A paradise Love will assure you,—
    True happiness, day after day.

The banner of Fame may wave o'er you,
    And fortune strew plenty around ;
But the heart that will ever adore you
    Is the fairest pearl ever was found !

Through sunlight, and storm, and affliction,
　　Through sickness and sorrow and Death,
Pure Love is no ideal fiction,
　　But real till Life's latest breath !

It shines like the Polar star o'er us,—
　　Encircling our being with bliss ;
It makes Life one rapturous chorus,
　　And links yonder bright world with this.

Oh, boon, so divine, true and holy !
　　Oh, spark that will ever endure !
In palace, or cottage, so lowly,
　　It shines ever constant and pure.

It leadeth our steps, which here darken,
　　To mansions of glory above ;
Oh, Love, unto you will I harken,
　　Sure guide unto God, who is Love !

SNOW.

A N ashen sky, and winds at rest ;
    Like strips of steel the brooks ;
Black boughs that fringe the woodland's crest ;
    Dead leaves in wayside nooks.
Brown fields all shorn and desolate ;
Heap high the fire, and click the gate ;
        For clouds of gray
        Now plainly say :
  " Ere the dawn there will be snowing."

    A sky of blue, a world of white,
      And winds that whistle shrill,
    The jolly coasters to invite
      Out on the glistening hill.
    New Life to thrill the crispy air ;
    New gold of sunshine everywhere ;
        And bright eyes say :
        " There's fun to-day,
  And the snow will soon be going."

THE DAYS.

OH, the cheery days of Spring
      When the budding woods are ringing,
And the brooklet, on the lea,
Like a child, with speech let free,
At its own wild, merry will
            Is singing !

Oh, the pleasant Summer days
   When the buds have found completeness,
And the flowers are drowsed in balm,
And the lake is lapt in calm,
And music crowds the hours
            With sweetness !

Oh, the days so golden, sad,
   When the birds are Southward calling,
And the amber sheaves of wheat
Surge around the reaper's feet,
And the red and topaz leaves
            Are falling !

Oh, the days so white and bleak,
   When the bitter winds are roving
In a hundred wayward moods,
Up and down the withered woods,—
Sad are these without thy heart
            So loving !

MEMORIAL DAY.

(1895.)

AGAIN we stand beside your graves,
　　Oh, comrades of the long ago !
The starry flag above us waves
　　Resplendent to and fro.
We twine a garland for the true,
　　The brave who passed away;
With blossoms of red, white and blue,
　　Keep we Memorial Day !

The sacred trust, till time shall end,
　　From us shall ne'er depart;
Where lie the brave, our feet shall wend,
　　With homage from each heart !
One thought—for us they gave their life !
　　Oh, flowers that softly sway,
For them sweet rest, surcease from strife,
　　Guard their Memorial Day !

Hark ! o'er the land, from shore to shore,
　　The tramp of comrades old !
Wreathe roses for the brave once more,
　　Their graves with bloom enfold !

On all alike, your benison
　Descends, fair skies of May !
Live in the hearts of everyone
　Our grand Memorial Day !

Oh, kindly hands that softly strew
　With sweetest buds and flowers,
These graves where rest the brave, the true,
　The comrades dear of ours.
Think not their spirits can forget,
　Though early passed away;
We'll meet beyond all sad regret,
　On God's Memorial Day !

THE REASON WHY.

OH, lovely are her costumes
　　That she wears with queenly pride;
And charming is her beauty,—
　That has never been denied;
Bewitching are her graces
　And her "fin de circle" air;
But still, to woo the maiden
　I never seem to care.

Not startled by her pertness,
　For her manners I admire;

Her *chic* is captivating,
   All a lover could desire;
But, there's another reason
   Why I worship her afar,
As a brooklet does the blossoms,
   As a bird the twilight star.

Yes, I gaze on her with rapture,
   But I dare not clasp her hand.
My lips are mute, while seated
   In her presence softly grand;
I'd like to breathe my passion,
   But, on me she'd have the laugh,—
I'm afraid of breach of promise,
   And she keeps a Phonograph !

THINE EYES.

I.

I GAZED within those melting deeps,
   And all the world to me
Seemed one sweet dream of Paradise,
   Joy, Peace and Melody!
The sadness of a Life had past,
And bliss supreme was mine, at last,
   Because of those dear eyes.

II.

As in some lake, so calm, so still,
  That holds, reflected clear,
The stars, the trees upon its marge,
  The leaves and blossoms near,
With joy too sweet to contemplate,
So in those eyes I saw my fate,—
  In glory of thine eyes.

III.

We may not meet on earth again,—
  Like streams we parted are;
But thou wilt ever be to me
  Hope's radiant guiding star!
And in the Life that is to be,
The brightest glories I shall see
  In the Heaven of thine eyes.

APART FROM THEE!

DAWN is not dawn unto the eyes
    That look alone on splendors rare,—
The roseate deeps of eastern skies,
    The dew, the roses sweet and fair,
        Apart from thee!

Night is not night, though in its deeps
    The myriad stars their splendor show ;
The heart is desolate that keeps
    Its watch, the pangs of love to know,
        Apart from thee !

The day glides on its weary course,
    And memory alone can weave,
Out of the present's dearth and loss,
    Its visions that awhile deceive,
        Apart from thee !

Old joys return, old thoughts that blest
    In happy hours when thou wast near ;
Oh, memories, so sweet, give rest,—
    Recall the Past, so vivid, clear,
        Apart from thee !

I would not wish to live Life's day,
    I will not joy to share its bliss,
If thou shouldst linger far away ;
    For all of Hope, Peace, Love I miss,
        Apart from thee !

A DREAM.

BEFORE an altar crowned with flowers
    Methought I stood one night ;
Blossoms of red and white and blue
    Shone gorgeous to my sight.

Upon the other side, unfurled,
    Our country's flag so true,
Its colors gleaming vividly,—
    The red, the white, the blue.

It brought me sad, sad memories,—
    This vision, of the Past,
Associations that throughout
    Eternity shall last,—

Linked with the child for aye beloved,
    Before God's altar now,
The diadem of Angels fair
    Resplendent on his brow.

And then a voice " Behold these flowers,
    They all shall fade and die,
Even as all who hear my words,
    Even, my friends, as I.

" But yonder Flag shall proudly wave
  To all eternity !
God's blessing on its starry folds
  The emblem of the Free !''

SEPARATION.

OH, tempest of the heart that loves !
    Where art thou now, my own ?
I gaze upon the jeweled stars,
    And know that I'm alone.
Oh, what a weary void is life
    When thou art from my side !
I drift, a hopeless, shattered wreck,
    Upon the tossing tide,
While separated thus from thee
A thousand ills encompass me.

There is no rest where thou art not,
    There is no peace,—my soul
Goes out to thee for solace sweet,—
    To thee, its Hope, its goal !
The night-wind syllables thy name,
    The stars recall those eyes
Wherein for me is every joy,—
    The light of Paradise !
And yet I know thy heart is true,
    As to the rose the gentle dew.

The glory of a Hope supreme
    Sustains me through the hour ;
The thought, the knowledge thou art mine,
    That joy at last, shall flower,—
The perfect bliss of meeting sweet
    With no dividing time,
Imparadising all of Life
    In ecstasy sublime !
For are our destinies not one ?
Shall they not blend ere Time be done ?

Oh, blessed Hope to still Life's storm !
    Oh, joy that is to be !
Love, perfect Love, hushes the heart
    As Christ did Galilee.
The night looks brighter for thy sake,
    I shall no more repine,
Trusting in thy dear Love that speaks
    Now to this heart of mine.
Not long shall separation mar,—
After the tempest, Lo ! the star !

WOMAN'S CLUBS.

A WOMAN'S club—the whirligig
Of time shows many changes;
But now the voice of womanhood
A brighter view arranges.
An atmosphere, a genial group,
Where sympathetic woman,
May have her sway, in glorious way,
In all that's good and human !

An interchange of all that's best
In Life, its mirth and gladness;
A circulation of all thought
To woo the heart from sadness.
In sooth, the brains of womanhood
As maid and wife and mother;
To represent this to the world
Our Mission, and no other !

As wife, with blessed influence
To wield now and forever !
To hold the links of love intact
That nothing can them sever.
As mother, holy trust from God,
So woman does her duty,
While goes the whirligig of Time,
In trustfulness and duty !

There is a voice that softly says
   The future is all glory !
The past is past,—for womanhood
   An old, forgotten story.
The simple recognition
   Of the sway that seeks forever
The bettering of human kind,
   Through woman's best endeavor.

The woman's Club—well let its aim
   Be still the world to brighten,—
To labor for the world at large,
   Its pains and ills to lighten.
To be the center of all good,
   The source of joy unbounded ;
To benefit the universe
   For this our clubs are founded.

CLOSE TO THE CROSS!

CLOSE to the Cross of Christ our Lord,—
  Oh, refuge sweet and dear!
Come, weary soul, with grief opprest,
  What balm, what comfort here.
    No other hope upon Life's sea,
    No purer, blest tranquility.
    Ave Maria, lead thou me
      Close to the Cross!

Close to the Cross that stands sublime
  Amid the wreck and doubt,—
The nameless ills of human Life,
  The snares within, without.
    Oh, Saviour of the world, to Thee
    I come on lowly bended knee!
    Ave Maria, watch o'er me,
      Close to the Cross!

Close to the Cross, there let me hide,
  And Death shall have no sting!
What need I fear of earthly pain
  While at its feet I cling?
    My willing soul I give to Thee
    To crown through all Eternity.
    Ave Maria, pray for me,
      Close to the Cross!

Close to the Cross, the True, the Blest !
  I lay Life's burdens down ;
Oh, Father, hear my humble prayer,
  Grant me the victor's crown !
    Protect, and aid, and comfort me ;
    Saviour of all, Thine would I be ;
    Ave Maria, guide thou me
      Close to the Cross !

THE NEW WOMAN.

SHE'S up to date in all that's fine,
  And has a charming style ;
For dash, she's in the foremost line,
  Old fogys at her smile.
We always read about her, now,
  And not about the new man ;
We all must tip the hat, and bow
  To her, the grand new woman !

CHORUS :

Fashions change, yes, everywhere,
  You scarce know what to do, man ;
She spends the cash, and cuts a dash,
  The elegant new woman !

She has a *chic* that's bound to strike,
  An independent air ;
How charmingly she rides a " bike,"
  No matter how folks stare !
Her "bloomers" show to all the world
  She's imitating you, man ;
Her banner's to the breeze unfurled,—
  The go-ahead, new woman !

Oh, how the dear old girls would stare,
  If they could see her now !
For critic man she doesn't care,
  Nor to his protest bow.
In fact, she is a wonder quite,
  Her "fads" are not a few, man,
And yet her little heart's all right,—
  This wonderful new woman !

www.ingramcontent.com/pod-product-compliance
Lightning Source LLC
Chambersburg PA
CBHW030827270326
41928CB00007B/934